Women and Contemporary Art in the Gulf

I0473535

Women and Contemporary Art in the Gulf offers a unique focus on the roles of women in contemporary art, cultural production and arts institutions in the Gulf.

Drawing on in-person experiences of the art and sites discussed, as well as research on regional artists and arts institutions, DeTurk argues that the Gulf Cooperation Council (GCC) countries of Bahrain, Kuwait, Oman, Qatar, Saudi Arabia and the United Arab Emirates have been largely excluded from the critical discourse about, and display of, contemporary Middle Eastern art. The book addresses this oversight by providing an examination of the work of several contemporary women artists from the Gulf region. DeTurk also discusses the role of women in museums and cultural institutions in the region, as well as the education systems available to emerging women artists. The discussion and analysis at the heart of the book connect to a range of larger themes, including the visual culture of patriarchy, connection to material culture and heritage, religious beliefs, trade and migration, rapid development, and the need to envision and create a post-oil economy.

Women and Contemporary Art in the Gulf, with its examination of the critical role women play in the formation of the cultural landscape of the Gulf, is an important contribution to discourse around the changing role of the GCC. It will be essential reading for scholars and students engaged in the study of art history, visual culture, museums and heritage, and women and gender studies.

Sabrina DeTurk, Ph.D., is a Lecturer in the Honors College at the University of Maine, Orono, Maine, USA. Her research interests include contemporary Middle Eastern art as well as the interplay between the Middle East and Venice in Renaissance art and architecture. Her work frequently considers issues of gender and social identity in visual culture.

Cultural Heritage, Art and Museums in the Middle East
Series Editors: Sarina Wakefield and Sabrina DeTurk

Cultural Heritage, Art and Museums in the Middle East book series includes volumes that address the ways in which representation and identity are connected to and implicated within cultural practice, broadly defined, in the global Middle East and provides in-depth studies that critically discuss and analyse this issue within the region. The series offers scope for emerging scholarship that takes a wider view of Middle Eastern Studies, by addressing Central Asia, Iran and the Middle Eastern diaspora. By doing so, the series aims to attract and support new directions in scholarship and provide a venue for those areas marginalised within this literature.

The series includes works that provide examples and interpretations of Middle Eastern cultural heritage, art and museums situated within a broader, global context. By highlighting these global connections, it aims to challenge the marginalisation of studies of the Middle East into the realm of regional studies. Further to this, the series critically explores how representation and identity are connected to cultural developments in the Middle East at various levels – local, national, regional, and transnational – in the fields of cultural heritage, art and museum studies. Titles in the series will provide much-needed resources and reference points for academics and students working in the fields of art, art history, anthropology, archaeology, cultural studies, critical heritage studies, Gulf Studies, Middle East Studies and museum studies. They will offer valuable insights for arts, heritage and museum practitioners; cultural policymakers; and others who have an interest in cultural production and practice within the Middle East.

Titles published in the series include:

Women and Contemporary Art in the Gulf
Identity, Institutions and Representation
Sabrina DeTurk

For more information about this series, please visit: https://www.routledge.com/Cultural-Heritage-Art-and-Museums-in-the-Middle-East/book-series/CHAMME

Women and Contemporary Art in the Gulf

Identity, Institutions and Representation

Sabrina DeTurk

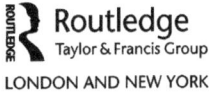

LONDON AND NEW YORK

First published 2023
by Routledge
4 Park Square, Milton Park, Abingdon, Oxon OX14 4RN

and by Routledge
605 Third Avenue, New York, NY 10158

Routledge is an imprint of the Taylor & Francis Group, an informa business

© 2023 Sabrina DeTurk

The right of Sabrina DeTurk to be identified as author of this work
has been asserted in accordance with sections 77 and 78 of the
Copyright, Designs and Patents Act 1988.

British Library Cataloguing-in-Publication Data
A catalogue record for this book is available from the British Library

ISBN: 978-1-032-05108-6 (hbk)
ISBN: 978-1-032-05335-6 (pbk)
ISBN: 978-1-003-19711-9 (ebk)

DOI: 10.4324/9781003197119

Typeset in Times New Roman
by codeMantra

Contents

Figures

Acknowledgments

I am grateful to the many artists and arts professionals in the Gulf region whose conversations during the years I lived in Dubai (2014–2021) provided both the impetus for writing this volume and much of the background information that shaped its development. I am particularly indebted to my students at Zayed University in the College of Arts and Creative Enterprises whose unfailing enthusiasm for the arts and commitment to their cultural and professional communities are inspirational. I also appreciate the institutional support of Zayed University during my time researching for this volume. While many at Zayed assisted in my work, I would like to particularly thank Hessa AlFahim for her assistance in the early research stages and Kara McKeown for her thoughtful reading and feedback on the manuscript. I would like to thank Dr Sarina Wakefield, my series co-editor, for her support and feedback throughout the writing process. Finally, I would like to thank my husband, Rick De Coyte, and daughter, Violet Beatrice DeTurk, for their unfailing support in this and all my endeavors.

Introduction

Context

Think of a woman artist from the Middle East ... who comes to mind? Shirin Neshat? Mona Hatoum? Emily Jacir? Chances are she is not a woman from the Gulf. Although women artists are active throughout the GCC countries of Bahrain, Kuwait, Oman, Qatar, Saudi Arabia and the United Arab Emirates there has been little substantive critical or art historical attention paid to these artists; indeed, even finding their work can be a challenge. The work of artists from the Middle East has seen increased exposure and analysis since the events of 9/11 and the Arab Spring through both exhibitions of contemporary art and renovations of Islamic art galleries at such high-profile Western institutions as the British Museum, the Louvre and the Metropolitan Museum of Art. Yet, as Nada Shabout (2015) asserts, these exhibitions and their related publications "do not cover the arts of the region equally [and] seem always to focus on countries subject to political instability and war. The reasons for the choice of countries range from media obsession to lack of access" (p. 54). The GCC countries, due to their status as predominantly peaceful Western allies and, with the possible exception of the UAE and Qatar, their lack of easily accessible art and cultural destinations, have been largely excluded from the critical discourse and display of contemporary Middle Eastern art. As Venetia Porter (2015), curator of Islamic and contemporary Middle East art at the British Museum, writes, for many curators

> a powerful draw of the work currently being produced by artists from or of the Middle East is that in its subject matter it appears to offer some insight into the complex and increasingly harrowing politics of the many countries that make up the region we call the Middle East.
>
> (pp. 203–205)

DOI: 10.4324/9781003197119-1

Thus, work produced by artists in more stable regimes is perhaps of less immediate or apparent interest to curators and collectors. Two of the British Museum's own important exhibitions seem to bear out this tendency: in the 2006 *Word into Art: Artists of the Modern Middle East* exhibition only three of the 78 included artists were from Gulf countries; by the time of 2021's *Reflections: Contemporary Art of the Middle East and North Africa* exhibition the percentage of Gulf artists had risen only slightly, to 14 out of 170 artists. If we accept the assertion by Jessica Winegar (2008) that "Through the selection, marketing, and consumption of particular kinds of art from the Middle East, American cultural elites have sought to create and sustain another [more positive] image of the region..." (p. 652) it makes sense that Western audiences might gravitate toward work produced by artists from countries in the current or recent conflict with the West, such as Afghanistan, Iran and Iraq.

It should be noted also that the Gulf countries, as relatively new nation-states, do not have the same historical depth of arts education and cultural organizations as are found in locations such as Baghdad, Cairo or Tehran, where art schools and artists' associations have long histories. Indeed, artists from the Gulf have at times traveled to study in other Middle Eastern art centers, including pioneering Emirati artist Najat Makki who in 1977 became the first woman to earn a government scholarship to study abroad, at the College of Fine Arts in Cairo (Meridian International Center, 2014). The first Arab art gallery in the Gulf, Sultan Gallery, opened in Kuwait in 1969; the Emirates Fine Arts Society was established in Sharjah in 1980; the Qatar Fine Arts Association was formed in the same year; Al-Meftaha Arts Village, an arts community in Saudi Arabia, was founded in 1989. The rapid rise of artists' organizations and museums and galleries in the Gulf did not begin until the late 1990s and early 2000s, meaning that the development of a culture of local exhibitions, arts education and cultural programming in Gulf communities is still in its relatively early stages. As Robert Kluijver (2013) writes in an essay surveying the contemporary art scene in the Gulf: "Contemporary art in the Gulf region is thus a new phenomenon; at the time of writing, it is hardly a decade old. This raises legitimate concerns about how connected it truly is to the region's culture" (p. 11). This nascent status likely also contributes to the lack of representation of Gulf artists in international exhibition venues. However, as Kluijver (2013) goes on to argue, "the Gulf contemporary visual arts scene is not only authentic, but also ... intricately linked to the historical cultural development of the region" (p. 11). Thus, it is critical that scholars, collectors and museum professionals with an interest in the arts of the Middle East give attention to the work coming out of the Gulf.

Although the exclusion of Gulf artists from international exhibitions arguably applies to most male artists as well, the fact that women artists in the Gulf are becoming as, if not more, prominent than their male counterparts within their countries of origin merits critical attention to their specific situation. One reason for the lack of attention to women artists from the Gulf on the part of international arts institutions may be the lack of travel opportunities for women in the region, particularly when such travel is to be undertaken alone for education or professional development. Saudi artist Manal Al Dowayan's 2011 work, *Suspended Together*, speaks specifically and poignantly to this situation. The installation consists of a "flock" of 200 porcelain and fiberglass doves, some suspended in mid-air and some on the ground. Each dove is imprinted with the permission document a Saudi woman needs to travel; the artist gathered specific documents from women educators, scientists, physicians and other professionals for this work, showing, in her words, that "regardless of age and achievement, when it comes to travel, all these women are treated like a flock of suspended doves" (Al Dowayan, n.d.). While guardianship laws vary across Gulf countries, with some less restrictive than Saudi, in all cases it is the cultural norm that women obtain permission from a male relative prior to travel and possibly require a male chaperone for any trips abroad. In a region where opportunities for arts education and viewing works of art (both contemporary and historic) remain fairly limited, this proscription on international travel both diminishes women artists' chances for professional growth and their ability to promote their own work internationally at exhibitions, biennials, art fairs and so on. To take one example, the 2006 exhibition *Without Boundary: Seventeen Ways of Looking*, curated by Fereshteh Daftari at the Museum of Modern Art in New York, featured 17 artists "who explore contemporary responses to Islamic art while also posing questions about issues of identity and spirituality" (MOMA, 2006). The curator specifically selected artists of Middle Eastern backgrounds but living in the West (alongside some American artists) for this exhibition. The group included no artists from Gulf countries; a perhaps unsurprising omission given that few artists from the Gulf region resided permanently in the West at the time (this is beginning to change). As countries in the Gulf begin to offer their own opportunities for higher education in the arts and to develop a cultural economy, including an internationally diverse gallery and museum sector, the exposure that women artists in the region have to the global art world is increasing, a change that can be seen in the careers of some of the women discussed in this volume.

Likewise, the critical work being done by women in the cultural and museum sectors receives limited attention outside the region and the strong participation by women in the BFA programs and private arts education initiatives in the Gulf is even less discussed. While this book cannot compensate for decades of inattention, it does pull together some major themes that I believe are central both to the cultural identity of *khaleejis* (Gulf Arabs) and to the work of contemporary women artists in the GCC. These include a visual culture of patriarchy, an intense connection to material culture and heritage, religious beliefs, trade and migration, rapid development, and the need to envision and create a post-oil economy. The arts and culture sector are key to that latter development and the attention being paid by regional leaders (at least nominally) to the empowerment of women is also critical to the emerging contemporary art scene in the region.

This book analyzes the work of several contemporary women artists from the Gulf and discusses the role of women in museums and cultural institutions in the region. Additionally, the book examines the education systems for emerging women artists in the Gulf, looking at national institutions, private universities and initiatives that seek to combine education, exhibition and community programming in the art and creative spheres. Throughout, I try to be mindful of Griselda Pollock's (1987) assertion that

> A central task for feminist art historians is ... to critique art history itself, not just as a way of writing about the art of the past, but as an institutionalized ideological practice that contributes to the reproduction of the social system by its offered images and interpretations of the world.
>
> (p. 3)

That is to say, I try to avoid reliance on dominant Western perceptions of Middle Eastern women or, in art historian Fran Lloyd's (2010) words "the monolithic and stereotypical media representations of Arab women who frequently were portrayed as passive, anonymous figures removed from the sphere of cultural production and from its histories" (p. 11). In discussing lesser-known women artists from the Gulf region, I attempt to rebalance the scales away from the predominant scholarly focus on women artists from more established artistic centers such as Baghdad, Beirut, Cairo and Tehran or from notably war-torn areas such as Palestine and Syria. By discussing the roles that women in the Gulf play in the cultural sector more broadly I hope to shed light on an important aspect of women's participation in cultural diplomacy. In looking at how education will shape the next generation of women artists and creative professionals in the region I offer a glimpse of the changes yet to come in this sphere. This is an intentionally short volume and in it I cannot begin to do full justice to the wide range of contemporary art practice and cultural participation by *khaleeji* women. The artists and arts professionals discussed here should be viewed as a representative sample, not an exhaustive survey, of the wide range of talented women at work in the region. Likewise, the images selected to accompany the text provide a small snapshot related to the themes addressed; however, the reader is encouraged to seek out examples of work by all the artists mentioned in the text. Many of them have excellent websites, often included in the references for each chapter. Additionally, online collections such as those of the British Museum, Barjeel Art Foundation and Edge of Arabia include works by several of the artists discussed. What I hope to accomplish in this volume is to spark the interest of readers to broaden the scope of research into an understudied area of contemporary art history and to raise questions and avenues for exploration by other critics and scholars, including emerging professionals from the Gulf region.

References

Al Dowayan, M. (n.d.). 'Artist's website'. [Online] Available at: https://www. manaldowayan.com [Accessed January 10, 2022].

Kluijver, R. (2013). *Contemporary Art in the Gulf: Context and Perspectives.* [Online] Available at: https://www.academia.edu/15269955/Contemporary_ Art_in_the_Gulf [Accessed January 20, 2022].

Lloyd, F. (2010). 'Revisiting Arab women's diasporic art practices in 1990s London'. *Middle East Institute Viewpoints: Creative Arab Women.* July 1, 2010. [Online] Available at: https://www.mei.edu/publications/introduction-state-arts-middle-east-volume-vi-creative-arab-women [Accessed January 13, 2022].

Meridian International Center. (2014). 'Past forward: Contemporary art from the emirates'. [Online] Available at: https://www.meridian.org/pastforward/ authors/najat-makki/ [Accessed January 20, 2022].

MOMA. (2006). 'Press release: *Without Boundary: Seventeen Ways of Looking*'. [Online] Available at: https://www.moma.org/calendar/exhibitions/83 [Accessed January 13, 2022].

Pollock, G. (1987). 'Women, art, and ideology: Questions for feminist art historians'. *Women's Studies Quarterly*, 15(1/2), pp. 2–9. Available at: https:// www.jstor.org/stable/40004832 [Accessed January 10, 2022].

Porter, V. (2015). 'Histories of the present: The changing worlds of Middle Eastern artists'. In Keshmirshekan, H. ed. *Contemporary Art from the Middle East: Regional Interactions with Global Art Discourses.* London: I.B. Tauris, pp. 203–219.

Shabout, N. (2015). 'Framing the discipline of contemporary art of the Arab world through the press'. In Keshmirshekan, H. ed. *Contemporary Art from the Middle East: Regional Interactions with Global Art Discourses.* London: I.B. Tauris, pp. 51–68.

Winegar, J. (2008). 'The humanity game: Art, Islam, and the war on terror'. *Anthropological Quarterly*, 81(3), pp. 651–681. Available at: https://www. jstor.org/stable/2548828 [Accessed January 10, 2022].

1 Heritage and National Identity

Gulf Heritage

To Westerners, the countries of the Gulf may appear to share a homogeneous heritage focused on Islam, desert, trade, tribal traditions and, more recently, oil. Nineteenth-century Orientalists repeated tropes of these heritage markers with their images of mosques, camels, caravanserai and harems. Even contemporary representations of the Gulf region, particularly in film and television, can be seen to lean heavily on standardized images of wealthy Arab men, oil fields and opulent palaces. The reality of Gulf heritage and identity is, however, far more complicated. As Ileana Baird (2021) describes, "Arabian identity … comprises a fabulous Arabia that has haunted the European imagination for the past three hundred years and a real Arabia that has had its unique history, culture, and traditions" (p. 4). There are, of course, many similarities between the religious and cultural histories of the GCC countries (Bahrain, Kuwait, Oman, Qatar, Saudi Arabia and the UAE) yet each state is fiercely protective of its national identity. Several scholars have recently explored the ways in which heritage practices in Gulf countries are inscribed in the art and museum landscapes of the region (Erskine-Loftus et al., 2019; Exell & Rico, 2014; Prager, 2015; Wakefield, 2020) and have drawn important connections between the realms of heritage, contemporary art and museology. This chapter considers specific women artists whose work responds to and, at times critiques, the heritage traditions of their home countries and region. Laila Prager (2015) asserts that "static [heritage] displays with their rigid labels and homogenizing categories are an expression of an authoritative discourse where the state exerts the main control over the meanings and symbols generated by the exhibitions" (p. 30). However, artists discussed in this chapter can use heritage to move beyond and problematize the static and authoritarian structures of

DOI: 10.4324/9781003197119-2

traditional displays through their contemporary practice. I argue that heritage serves both to anchor and to unsettle the work of these artists, particularly when considered through the lens of gender. The chapter concludes with a brief analysis of the gendered nature of many heritage sites in the region, through a discussion of the Bahrain Pearling Trail and Qasr Al Hosn (UAE).

Maha Malluh

Born in Saudi Arabia in 1959, Maha Malluh has gained prominence in the Gulf contemporary art scene with her large-scale installations created from discarded materials, notably metal dishes and cooking pots. The title *Food for Thought* is given to several of her works, some featuring dishes and pots and some crafted from old cassette tapes placed inside used wooden baking trays. The earliest of these works date from 2012 and were included in the *Edge of Arabia Jeddah: We Need to Talk* exhibition held at the Al Furisiya Marina and Mall in Jeddah during that year. Malluh exhibited four works in the show, two sculptures and a pair of photograms, taking her place amidst a roster of some of Saudi Arabia's foremost contemporary artists, such as Manal Al-Dowayan, Abdulnasser Gharem and Ahmed Mater. *We Need to Talk*, which was the first major public exhibition of contemporary Saudi art in Saudi Arabia, was curated by Mohamed Hafiz, who described the show as an invitation "to the audience to react, to think for themselves and to discuss how they can positively influence the world around them" (Mousawi, 2012, p. 10). The works by Malluh were featured in both the "Past" and "Future" sections of the exhibition; a fitting juxtaposition for an artist whose work both reflects and repurposes traditional objects, particularly those associated with food and dining. The baking trays, metal dishes and cooking pots that form the main raw materials for the sculptures in *Food for Thought* are taken out of their traditional context of family gatherings and shared meals and presented in towers that evoke the rapidly urbanizing landscape of Saudi Arabia. The baking trays no longer hold bread but are instead filled with obsolete cassette tapes featuring recordings of Islamic sermons, perhaps a nod to the displacement not only of cultural heritage but also of religious tradition in a modernizing Kingdom. One of the sculptures shown by Malluh in this exhibition, known now as *Food for Thought II* (2012), was acquired by the Tate Modern in London, and in a website entry describing that work and others by Malluh, Gaia Tedone (2013) notes that "These outmoded objects … convey the cultural and social tensions of a region negotiating a path between consumerism, modernity and its cultural heritage." Heritage for Maha Malluh becomes at once a site of cherished memory and of rupture and displacement, yet the careful repurposing of discarded objects can offer new possibilities for the conjunction of past and present. As Malluh says of her work, "When an object can no longer operate as was originally intended, a new function through 'adaptive reuse' may be the only way to preserve the heritage of its significance" (Mousawi, 2012, p. 77).

Malluh's work also references a heritage tradition significant in Saudi Arabia and throughout the Arab world, that of the spoken literary, specifically poetic, word. One iteration (in multiple versions) of her *Food for Thought* sculptures is titled *Food for Thought – Almuallaqat*, a reference to a collection of pre-Islamic odes that some traditions say were embroidered in gold and hung on the walls of the Ka'ba in Mecca. In Malluh's installations (versions of which featured in the inaugural exhibitions of both the Louvre Abu Dhabi and the Jameel Arts Center in Dubai), used aluminum cooking pots of various sizes are hung on the walls, blackened bottoms facing toward the viewer. The pots form a visual reminder of a long tradition of Bedouin hospitality as well as a reference to the unseen labor of countless women who tended the fires and made the meals that would be prepared in these vessels. For Malluh, however, the pots are intended to bridge a gap between the verbal and the visual, in which historically the visual has been considered second to the literary in Arab culture but which is today upended by the proliferation of imagery via social media and other forms of entertainment, accompanied by a declining interest in reading and literacy among the population. As Malluh writes:

> Thus, what this work calls out for is a reconnection with our literary heritage, but using the visual medium to do so in order to communicate with the rest of the world. Therefore, these hanging pots are both a salute to our literary heritage, as well as being a testament to our current need for everything visual. These pots speak of our revived archaeological search for our visual heritage, our culture that has been in the shadows of our literary heritage for so long. Without dismissing the significance and aesthetic beauty of the original muallaqat, this work both acknowledges the position poetry has in Arab culture and heritage, whilst simultaneously allowing for an engaging visual dialogue with the remainder of the world.

> (Malluh, 2014)

Malluh's unique interweaving of the verbal and the visual speaks to an ongoing desire to connect with and reshape heritage sources in ways that speak to contemporary issues in Saudi Arabia and the Gulf region. Through her mixed-media sculptural installations, Malluh draws on the material culture of the Kingdom in order to engage with a global conversation about heritage, tradition and development.

Dana Awartani

If Maha Malluh's sculptures provoke a conversation about the multiple, and sometimes conflicting, ways in which contemporary Gulf citizens engage with their past, the work of Dana Awartani (born 1987) offers a more immediately recognizable homage to past artistic traditions and techniques. Awartani identifies as being of mixed heritage, including Saudi, Syrian, Palestinian and Jordanian roots, but was born and lives in Jeddah, Saudi Arabia. Trained initially at Central Saint Martin's, with a Master's degree in Traditional Arts from the Prince's School in London, Awartani specializes in geometric design which she embodies in painting, sculpture and mixed-media installations. An analysis of two of Awartani's works will show that, despite the surface reliance on traditional forms of Islamic patterns, the artist engages with present dilemmas of unchecked growth and heritage destruction while simultaneously bringing the historically grounded visual identity of Islamic culture to the forefront.

In a series of eight works on paper, *The Islamic Caliphates* (2016, now in the collection of the British Museum), Awartani uses gold leaf, ink and gouache to create stages of a design reminiscent of Quranic illumination. In the first piece (*al Khulafa' al-Rashidun*), the inked grid underlaying the pattern is predominantly visible, with only a gold leaf circle indicating the start of an illumination; by the final page (*Ottoman*), the full pattern is revealed in striking tones of blue, red, gold and green. The titles of each piece allude to the progression of Islamic caliphates from the time of the Prophet's death through the Ottoman period; the series as a whole

> explores how each of the historical civilizations have contributed to this art form, building out from an illuminated core in layers. This piece also dually depicts the geographical expansion of the religion of Islam over time, starting from the gold circle which represents the birth of the religion in the Hejaz, all the way through to its peak which spans from the far East across to Europe which is portrayed in the final 'shamsa'.
>
> (Awartani, 2022)

The work also connects to the artist's own experience of slowly building the skills required of a master illuminator (to obtain her *Ijazah* certificate), a process of craftsmanship she views as integral to her practice and one honed during her time at the Prince's School:

> I fell in love with the discipline of the traditional arts because it's not something you learn overnight or from a one-week course, it takes years of training and I was just really drawn to the way of learning the arts – the process. It's humbly training under a master and it's also about keeping that tradition alive that, sometimes, a family would do for generations.
>
> (Shehmir, 2022)

While works such as *The Islamic Caliphates* pay a direct homage to the traditional skills of the masters of illumination in the Islamic world, Awartani's mixed-media installation, *I Went Away and Forgot You. A While Ago I Remembered. I Remembered I'd Forgotten You. I Was Dreaming.* (2017), both celebrates that traditional craft and mourns its destruction and loss. For this piece, Awartani meticulously crafted a large-scale pattern out of hand-colored sand on the floor of an abandoned house in the old part of Jeddah, the area where the artist's grandparents used to live. Once the painstaking construction of this detailed work was completed, the artist filmed herself sweeping away the sand, thus destroying the pattern; this recorded act was staged

> as a symbolic commentary on the modern-day destruction of our cultural identity and heritage, which has been a result of a careless and an obsessive need for a more modernized and industrial society without the conscious awareness of what we are leaving behind.
>
> (Awartani, 2022)

Through her actions, the artist called attention to the losses incurred by modernization and issued a plea for greater consideration of keeping the past, present and future in co-existence rather than simply destroying one to make way for the next.

Noor Abuissa

Qatari artist Noor Abuissa (born 1989) is, like Dana Awartani, inspired by the profusion of color and pattern found in Islamic decorative arts, as well as in manuscript illumination and architecture. Unlike Awartani, whose focus on craftsmanship often leads to intricate realizations of patterned form, Abuissa explodes those patterns into colorful canvases and sculptural installations, evoking the past but also creating a contemporary aesthetic. Her shaped canvases recall at once the geometric patterns of Islamic heritage and the experiments of the Abstract Expressionists. Her sculptures utilize familiar motifs from the Gulf, such as the patterns of *mashrabiya* panels, but also have an affinity with the works of Minimalist artists of the 1960s and 1970s. Abuissa's work focuses not on the whole at the expense of its parts but rather on the interplay between the two, capturing, as the artist says, "the small moments that bring us joy as well as big experiences that might define us" (Abuissa, 2019).

In her repurposing of a heritage tradition to suit contemporary tastes, Abuissa also demonstrates herself a master of the multiple roles that many artists must now assume as part of their creative identity: marketer, brand ambassador and salesman. Her website offers opportunities for commissions as well as works for sale and her carefully curated Instagram feed highlights her connection to projects such as the 2018 "Dhow Art" challenge and exhibition sponsored by Red Bull, in which Abuissa was one of six artists selected to create a work on a replica of the traditional Gulf sailing craft. In this regard, Abuissa bridges the worlds of commerce, entertainment and fine art in a way that seems congruent with the growing emphasis in Gulf countries on art and design as a driver of economic growth in a post-oil economy. As more women artists come of age in the region, they may find that the merging of traditional exhibitions in museums and galleries with exposure through social media and commercially sponsored exhibition opportunities gives them the greatest range of appreciation for their work.

A 2020 installation at Alfardan Medical with Northwestern Medicine (AMDN), an ambulatory care center in Lusail, Qatar, offers an example both of Abuissa's signature style and the type of partnership that can result in significant exposure for the work of emerging Gulf artists. *Relformation* (2020) is a large-scale installation of Abuissa's colorful, geometric wall sculptures, commissioned by Emergeeast, an online gallery and art consultancy founded and led by Dima Abdul Kader and Nikki Meftah in Dubai in 2014. *Relformation* features a profusion of triangular shapes, in various bright hues, configured as though shifting and dancing across the walls in much the way light is refracted through stained glass. It is a bright and eye-pleasing work, appropriate to its setting in a public space within a healthcare setting. That its placement there was facilitated by two self-described "third culture kids," with ties to the Middle East and the UK, whose interest in championing the work of young, Middle Eastern artists led to the formation of the Emergeeast platform, speaks to the new way of forging connections and conducting the business of art in the Gulf region (Esfandiari, 2021). That the participants in this exchange were all women speaks to the increasingly prominent role they are playing in that business.

Bouthayna Al Muftah

An artist working at the intersection of performance, painting and calligraphy, Bouthayna Al Muftah (born 1987), is a Qatari whose arts education was enabled by her country's bid to welcome branch campuses of Western institutions of higher education – in Al Muftah's case, the Virginia Commonwealth University School of the Arts. Al Muftah graduated from VCU Qatar in 2009 with a bachelor's degree in graphic design and has developed an expressive, calligraphic style of working primarily in black ink on paper. Her works range from stylized portraits to text rendered in an imagistic style to fully abstract, geometric forms. Of particular interest in the context of this chapter is Al Muftah's connection to Qatari folklore and to calligraphic forms, both on view in the projects described here.

In 2018, Al Muftah created the exhibition *Echoes* in Project Space 12 at Mathaf Arab Museum of Modern Art in Doha. This complex and multifaceted installation, curated by Fatma Mostafawi, featured printmaking, painting, bookbinding and performance/video to

> reflect on the rapid social and cultural changes that have taken place in her surroundings in a short period of time [and] to evoke shared local memories and question current local cultural practices visibly influenced by technology with growing focus on individualism.
>
> (Mathaf, 2020)

To create the work, Al Muftah relied and reflected on the stories and memories she has collected from locals, specifically evoking a child's game – 'tag 'tag 'tagya – which she "deconstructs" to "redefine cultural narratives, offering a symbolic experience in a space in which the past and the present intersect" (Mathaf, 2020). One component of this deconstruction was the creation of a pen and ink work on the floor of the gallery, the process of which Al Muftah documented in video. In this process, which echoes performative gestures as varied as action painting and the creation of sand mandalas, Al Muftah utilized natural materials and her own body to create a circular motif which anchored the center of the gallery. After inscribing a circular text with pen and ink at the center of the work, she dipped a brush made of twigs in black ink and used a sweeping motion to encircle the text with strokes of varied size and density. Finally, coating her feet with ink, she walked lightly around the text and brushstrokes, inscribing her physical presence on the work while simultaneously evoking the actions of playing children. Writing of performance art in the Gulf, Cristiana de Marchi (2016) notes that such works are rarely performed in front of audiences and that the artist's body "becomes a tool – an instrument for measuring time and space" in the context of both the performance and documentation of the work. Al Muftah's performance and subsequent video documentation, as well as the ephemeral work on the gallery floor, may be seen as measuring the time and space of her own childhood, as well as the rapidly evolving culture that surrounds her.

While works such as *Echoes* place Al Muftah in the company of artists who seek to interrogate heritage and changing traditions through the lens of contemporary art, her collaboration with fashion designer Yasmin Mansour situates her work in the context of the overlap between culture and commerce that we saw with Noor Abuissa's contribution to Red Bull's Dhow Art exhibition. At the 2021 Fashion Trust Arabia awards, event co-chair HE Sheikha Al Mayassa bint Hamad bin Khalifa Al Thani wore an abaya designed by Mansour and made of fabric covered with loose, slightly abstract Arabic calligraphy created by Al Muftah, similar in style to the text used in her artworks. In addition to her role with the Fashion Trust, Sheikha Al Mayassa, who is the sister of the ruling emir of Qatar, chairs Qatar Museums, a position that has earned her a reputation as a significant patron and shaper of arts and culture in the Middle East and beyond. The abaya designed by Mansour and Al Muftah was thus a fitting symbol of the Sheikha's connections to the worlds of both fashion and art, a connection that is increasingly apparent throughout the landscape of contemporary art and in the global art market. Sheikha Al Mayassa's remarks at the 2021 FTA awards ceremony highlighted the creative tension between innovation and tradition as she urged young designers to "find the voice that will make you stand out from the crowd" but also "to remain true to their origins" and "to delve into their past to find the contemporary" (Dib & Hadiyah, 2021), advice that may apply equally to artists such as Al Muftah, whose work navigates the spaces between tradition and change.

Maitha Demithan (UAE)

Emirati artist Maitha Demithan (born 1989) has moved in and out of public view in the years since her graduation from Zayed University in 2008, with a degree in fine art. In 2009, she had her first exhibition at Tashkeel in Dubai where she debuted work using scanography, a process of creating photographic prints from layered images captured with a flatbed scanner. These early portraits did not always feature actual scans of the people the works represented; *Ummi* (mother in Arabic), for example, is created from repeated scans of a burqa, the traditional Emirati face mask worn by women of older generations. As her work developed, Demithan began to ask friends and relatives to participate in her process by having their likeness captured on her scanner. The artist explains that she prefers to work with familiar sitters: "I like to scan people I know and feel a connection with. I would not feel comfortable with a stranger, unless I did a few sittings and felt that it was going well" (Bedirian, 2020) and her images have an intimate quality that is suited to the practice of working largely with close associates.

In 2014, Demithan participated in a residency at the Delfina Foundation in London and presented her solo show, *Mutajadid*, at Tashkeel. Her works, continuing in the scanographic technique, mixed images of people with heritage objects, particularly clothing, to create a portrait of the artist's family and culture and of the Emirates at large. The following years saw participation in fewer exhibitions, but in 2017, an image by Demithan, *Mother*, was featured prominently in the traveling exhibition *I Am*, sponsored by the inter-faith NGO Caravan. The 31 participating artists came from both Muslim and Christian backgrounds and the exhibition highlighted the

> insights and experiences of Middle Eastern women as they confront issues of culture, religion and social reality in a rapidly changing world both in the Middle East and West ... challeng[ing] existing stereotypes and misconceptions about Middle Eastern women by showing how they dynamically and very significantly contribute to the fabric of local and global culture.

> (Caravan, n.d.)

Demithan's work was an unusual self-portrait, in which the artist scanned herself holding a camera and two of her young children. She spoke of the vulnerability inherent in such an image:

> Since I've become a mother, I've found it extremely hard to make time, or spend time creatively. It made me feel helpless, and doubt myself as a mother – because sometimes I yearn to work on my art. It was a courageous step for me to create *Mother* because it is showing the world a vulnerable side of me which I am new to. But it's a message to prove that I am both a mother and an artist.

(East, 2017)

It is unusual for women artists in the Gulf to speak so openly about the conflicting demands of motherhood and career. Demithan's forthrightness, and continued presence in the visual arts scene in Dubai (her work was featured in a major PR campaign urging residents to "stay home" during the COVID-19 lockdown, and she created work for EXPO 2020), may help to create a space for younger women artists to have the honest and difficult conversations about balancing work and family that are critically needed in the region.

Amani Al-Thuwaini

The traditional art of *sadu* weaving is merged with reflections on marriage and dowries in the work of Kuwaiti mixed-media artist Amani Al-Thuwaini (born 1989). Al-Thuwaini is of mixed Ukrainian and Kuwaiti heritage, and aspects of both cultures have influenced her work; likewise, the cultural similarities of textile traditions and elaborate marriage rituals are evidenced in the artist's embroideries and mixed-media sculptures. Two works particularly reference marriage and dowries while also drawing on traditions of female handicrafts: *Dazza* (2016) and *Staged* (2020). The earlier piece, *Dazza*, combines sadu weaving with a vinyl sculpture in the form of a Chanel handbag, placed together in a rectangular form invoking a kilim or wall-hanging. As Al-Thuwaini describes it:

> *Dazza* [Arabic for dowry] as a tradition, used to be very ceremonial in the early days of Kuwait. After globalization and modernism, this evolved and emphasized the display of objects more through the inclusion of international designer goods within the

dowry. Material transformation is undeniable, and this is what the piece symbolizes. Sadu weaving represents tradition, and the leather section resembles an oversized Chanel bag. The Chanel bag is used as a symbol as it is actually included in a lot of contemporary dowries. The brand logo was replaced with the Arabic word 'Dazza' in gold color plexiglass.

(Al-Thuwaini, n.d.)

The work thus inscribes a contemporary change to a traditional practice (the inclusion of luxury, branded goods within a bride's dowry) within a heritage art (sadu). This wrapping, or perhaps interlacing, of tradition and modernity is reflective of the rapid pace of social change in the Gulf while also indicating a desire to retain certain traditions.

Al-Thuwaini's 2020 embroidered work, *Staged*, shows the elaborate preparations and rituals of a Kuwaiti wedding, a practice that would be recognizable in any Gulf society. The bride and her guests are attended to throughout by a myriad of helpers, figures which the artist has rendered in gold thread, a choice that she describes as being

made to highlight the presence of the normally-unnoticed helpers who make the event possible to the smallest detail. By shedding light on the unseen and 'the other', I emphasise how local traditions are often challenged by the craving for opulence.

(Al-Thuwaini, n.d.)

Interestingly, Al-Thuwaini connects the helpers with "local traditions," whereas they are most likely domestic workers from Southeast Asian countries, not Kuwaitis. The artist herself notes this reality in an interview with *Bomb* magazine, where she explains that

I'm playing with hierarchy, with who's important and who's getting the attention. Weddings in Kuwait are large, elaborate affairs, and they need many workers. The people who do the work are often immigrants, and they're usually underpaid and looked down on. There's a lot of discrimination based on race and economic status.

(Bomb, 2020)

A possible reading of the work, then, positions Kuwait heritage traditions in the same liminal space as immigrant laborers, necessary but unrecognized. Through her work, Al-Thuwaini seeks to bring attention to those neglected practices and to question the consumerist nature of contemporary Kuwaiti society.

Aseel AlYaqoub

Aseel AlYaqoub (born 1986) is a Kuwaiti multi-disciplinary and research-based artist whose work frequently interrogates the ways in which the nation-state seeks to shape collective memory and perceptions of culture, heritage and history. Working across sculpture, video, drawing and printmaking, the artist often utilizes found objects and documents to analyze what is shown and hidden in state-sanctioned narratives of progress. In her words,

> In the process of assembling and destroying this inventory of found materials, my goal is to discern why some historical elements fit well within the national narrative, while others are deliberately forgotten. Their synthesis is translated into new constructions in the form of videos, drawings, installations and prints to re-evaluate the nation's processes of self-identification and state-making, happening within pressure-cooker conditions, post-imperial dissolution and re-attachment.
>
> (AlYaqoub, n.d.)

Her M.F.A. thesis exhibition, held at Pratt Institute in New York in 2015 and titled *Popular Games*, featured several works of sculpture and video that addressed the artificial delineation and reconfiguration of Kuwait throughout its recent history. Framed as a "game" or "epic adventure," the artist satirically encapsulated the contrived development of the emirate as a set of "rules" for engagement. Examples include:

> Allow the British to draw a small nation with a red pen. Call it Kuwait. Call the British to help extract oil. Once the Americans are interested, call them. Sell lots of oil. Import architects and urban planners. *Bonus points if they are Scandinavian.* Demolish existing mud-wall borders to make room for infrastructure. Fill the gaps with highways. Tear down mud houses – replace with incongruous mansions. Create foundations in the form of heritage

institutions and cultural festivals. Infuse nationalism and patri-
otism into the citizens. Continuously project cultural themes on
modern media as national political culture. Invent cultural tradition. State-sponsor everything you can. Control the perception of
history. Continue nation building.

(AlYaqoub, n.d.)

These directives, while representative of Kuwait in AlYaqoub's work,
could be applied to virtually any Gulf state and to many other countries where the construction or reconstruction of cultural memory has
become a state-sponsored project.

AlYaqoub has continued to grapple with questions of colonialism,
identity and the role of the state in constructing cultural memory,
seen also in her work for the exhibition *Stories We Tell Ourselves*,
curated by Matthew Kyba and held in 2021 at the Foreman Gallery
of Bishop's University in Quebec, Canada. For the exhibition,
AlYaqoub produced a series of drawings titled *Imagining the
Imagined in the Imaginary* (2021) that reconstruct artifacts from the
First National Museum of Kuwait, which was severely damaged
during the 1990 Iraqi invasion of Kuwait. According to curator
Matthew Kyba (2021),

Sourced purely from found documentation of its cultural spaces,
AlYaqoub's pencil silhouettes offer glimpses of a museum that
no longer exists. These items will continue to haunt how the
country's national museum system — a system understood
within Eurocentric (and Western-dominated) communities as an
important institution for showcasing domestically held cultural
artifacts — will be defined in the long term.

AlYaqoub thus engages in conversation both about the construction
of history and memory within her homeland of Kuwait and with the
global dialog around decolonization and the relevance of Western ide-
ological and institutional constructs to the Global South.

Heritage Sites: Bahrain Pearling Pathway and
Qasr Al Hosn (UAE)

The intersection of gender and tradition as inscribed in heritage sites
throughout the Gulf region is a topic in need of further research.
Here, I touch on those intersections as seen in two recent heritage

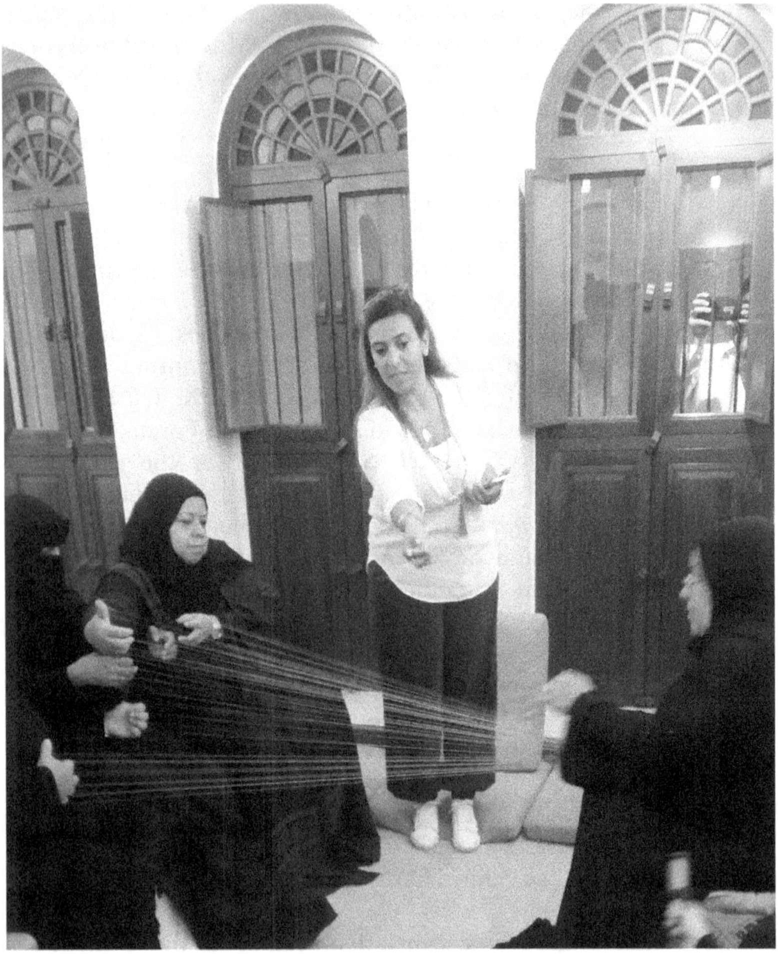

Figure 1.1 A group of Bahraini women demonstrating embroidery in one of the houses along the Pearling Path. Photograph by the author.

preservation projects: the Pearling Pathway in Muharraq, Bahrain and Qasr Al Hosn in Abu Dhabi, UAE. Both sites draw on the expertise of both local and expatriate female museum and heritage professionals, and each embodies elements of women's historical and contemporary lived experience in its structures, programming and marketing.

Bahrain Pearling Path

In 2012, the project "Pearling, Testimony of an Island Economy" became the second recognized UNESCO World Heritage site in Bahrain. Comprising a series of "15 property components: three vast oyster beds located in the northern territorial waters of Bahrain, one seashore site at the southern tip of Bahrain's Muharraq Island, and nine clusters of historic buildings consisting of seventeen architectural structures embedded in the urban fabric of Muharraq city" (BACA, n.d.), the project is known as the "Pearling Path" and centers on a 3.5 km path through the key structures, emphasizing pearling as a "grand narrative [that] remains the most significant source of Bahraini cultural identity" (BACA, n.d.). Although pearling was practiced in other Gulf countries, notably Qatar and the UAE, from the 1850s to the 1930s, Bahrain "built itself and its reputation around the pursuit of pearls, powering the country's economy and shaping its culture, social structures and national identity" (Mollard, 2020, p. 29). Pearling was an exclusively male pursuit, yet the cyclical nature of the profession – the pearling dhows would leave each summer for months at a time – ensured that for a significant stretch of the year Muharraq became, effectively, a city of women.

The Pearling Path project incorporates both the restoration of historic structures and the construction of new ones, including two visitors' centers and a multistorey car park. Also integral to the project are a series of public squares created in the areas where buildings were demolished, "welcome places of respite, unsuspected as you turn a corner and envisioned as chance encounters between residents and visitors" (Mollard, 2020, p. 30). These squares are emblematic of a desire on the part of the project's sponsor, the Bahrain Authority for Culture and Antiquities (BACA), to, as described by Noura Al Sayeh, Head of Architectural Affairs at BACA, "serve the local community and to reverse years of neglect and lack of maintenance" in the Muharraq neighborhood (Mollard, 2020, p. 31). Following the demise of the pearling industry, Muharraq became a center largely for single, male migrant workers; the restoration project seeks to encourage families back to the neighborhood for both cultural programming associated with the Pearling Path and permanent residence in improved family homes.

The interest in preserving and highlighting women's roles within the neighborhood is seen not only through the desire to provide public spaces and programming that attracts women and children to the project but also through the specific inclusion of a structure and exhibition designed to "explore the female perspective on the pearling economy" (BACA, n.d.). The Shaheen bin Saqir bin Mohammed Al-Jalahma House is one of the structures slated for conservation as part of the South Conservation and Rehabilitation component of the project. Described as a "large, complex residence in which women, as a result of multiple marriages, made up the majority of household members" (BACA, n.d.), the Al-Jalahma House offers a view into the gender-segregated spaces of Islamic residential architecture. Yet, it also suggests the ways in which the particular nature of Bahraini pearling society allowed for flexibility in gender roles and spatial occupation: "… reception areas for men, for example, would revert to female domains once male visitors left" (BACA, n.d.). Unlike other structures on the Pearling Path, for example, the Murad Majlis (which still serves a private space for male members of that family) or the Siyadi Majlis, which are permanently encoded as male spaces, structurally separate from the female areas of the home, the Al-Jalahma House affords an alternative configuration of private space that accounts for the prominent position of women within the social structure of a late nineteenth- and early twentieth-century pearling society.

Qasr Al Hosn

In Abu Dhabi, UAE, the Qasr Al Hosn site has been occupied since the late 1700s, when the city's watchtower was constructed. The original structure was expanded in the ensuing years and has served as fort, palace, government seat and national archive. Following an extensive, multi-year renovation program, it re-opened as a museum in 2018 and is now described as "the nation's living memorial and the narrator of Abu Dhabi's history" (Qasr Al Hosn, 2019). In its original iterations, Qasr Al Hosn would have been a strictly gender-segregated space; in its current state, like some of the structures of Bahrain's Pearling Path, the complex seeks to engage women and families in an exploration of UAE's national and cultural identity.

Two aspects in particular speak to this engagement with women as a defining strategy of Qasr Al Hosn's design and programming: an impressive and much-heralded exhibition of Emirati fashion held in 2020–2021 and the permanent House of Artisans exhibition which opened in 2021. "Fashion Through the Years," on display from December 2020 through February 2021, featured examples of Emirati dress with a focus on the decades from the 1940s through the 1980s, not coincidentally the same decades surrounding the growth of an oil-based economy and the unification of the country. The exhibition surveyed both men's and women's fashion and adornment, but the emphasis was largely on women's dress and jewelry, ranging from traditional items to European-inspired designs. The exhibition was constructed as a social history of the UAE, and particularly of Abu Dhabi, with a focus on the ways in which changing garments reflected the cultural changes of the nation. As described by Salama Al Shamsi, Director of Qasr Al Hosn,

> the exhibition showcases the cultural significance of fashion in the emirate during the crucial four decades of development and nation-building and provid[es] a unique opportunity to explore clothing trends and methods of personal expression from decades ago. Visitors will be transported back in time to connect with the experiences of our ancestors and gain deeper insight into the UAE's rich heritage.
>
> (DCT, 2020)

The inclusion of important pieces of jewelry, such as necklaces once belonging to Her Highness Sheikha Fatima bint Mubarak Al Ketbi, wife of Sheikh Zayed and known as "Mother of the Nation," signaled the important role that female adornment plays in Emirati society. As Marie-Claire Bakker and Kara McKeown (2021) write in their study of jewelry in the Arabian Gulf, "The relationship of an Arab woman with her jewelry is both public and private and it is an intrinsic part of her identity" (p. 195). The exhibit at Qasr Al Hosn thus showcased not only the transitory nature of fashion trends and changes over the years but also the enduring relevance of women's dress in both individual and collective constructions of identity.

The items on display in "Fashion Through the Years" also high-lighted the craftsmanship of those who made them, an emphasis that forms the central conceit of the permanent House of Artisans exhibit that opened in spring 2021 at Qasr Al Hosn. Developed to showcase and preserve the tangible and intangible cultural heritage of Emirati craftsmanship, the House of Artisans particularly focuses on the crafts of *sadu* (weaving), *talli* (embroidery) and *khoos* (palm frond weaving), all of which are practiced by women. Male-dominated crafts such as those associated with the maritime trade, as well as perfumery, are also represented but the emphasis is on the work of female artisans. One such traditional practice, *sadu*, which is the weaving of goat hair that Bedouin women used to make tent dividers, cushions and other decorative elements of the nomadic lifestyle, has been placed on the UNESCO List of Intangible Cultural Heritage in

Need of Urgent Safeguarding. *Sadu* is not only a gendered activity, in that it is a craft practiced only by women, but also reflects in the gendered spaces of Bedouin life: "the separation created by a tent divider affects people's behavior and the way they move: the materiality of the space impacts the fluidity of their movement and the rhythm of their navigation through different parts of the home" (Al-Ogayyel & Oskay, 2021, p. 146).

Al Shamsi notes the importance of developing younger artisans with skills in these traditional crafts:

> What we strive to do as part of our initiatives and programmes is to include younger artisans to practice their skill in the most authentic way. We try to move [the skill set] from one generation to the other through workshops and training.
>
> (Faruque, 2021)

Initiatives underway at the House of Artisans that are designed to further stimulate interest in traditional craft and to spread it beyond the boundaries of specialized practitioners include workshops with university students in arts and design majors and the production of contemporary design items (such as handbags, jewelry and homewares) that incorporate elements of traditional technique with modern styles and materials. Through the safeguarding and dissemination of women's craftsmanship, Qasr Al Hosn provides an example of how specifically female activities, and their associated spaces, can become an integral part of heritage preservation and interpretation.

References

Abuissa, N. (2019). 'Artist's website'. [Online] Available at: https://www.noorabuissa.com/ [Accessed January 4, 2022].

Al-Ogayyel, R. and Oskay, C. (2021). '*Al-Sadu* weaving: Significance and circulation in the Arabian gulf'. In Baird, I. and Yağcioğlu, H. eds. *All Things Arabia: Arabian Identity and Material Culture.* Leiden and Boston: Brill, pp. 143–162.

Al-Thuwaini, A. (n.d.). 'Artist's website'. [Online] Available at: http://amanialthuwaini.com/ [Accessed January 24, 2022].

AlYaqoub, A. (n.d.). 'Artist's website'. [Online] Available at: https://aseelalyaqoub.com/ [Accessed January 26, 2022].

Awartani, D. (2022). 'Artist's website'. [Online] Available at: https://danaawartani.com/ [Accessed January 4, 2022].

Bahrain Authority for Culture and Antiquities. (n.d.). 'Pearling path'. [Online] Available at: https://pearlingpath.bh/en/ [Accessed January 7, 2022].

Baird, I. (2021). 'Introduction: Complex legacies: Materiality, memory, and myth in the Arabian Peninsula'. In Baird, I. and Yağcioğlu, H. eds. *All Things Arabia: Arabian Identity and Material Culture*. Leiden and Boston: Brill, pp. 1–19.

Bakker, M. and McKeown, K. (2021). 'From cradle to grave: A life story in jewelry'. In Baird, I. and Yağcioğlu, H. eds. *All Things Arabia: Arabian Identity and Material Culture*. Leiden and Boston: Brill, pp. 191–212.

Bedirian, R. (2020). 'Why Maitha Demithan hasn't yet seen her striking #StayHome artworks on Sheikh Zayed Road'. *The National*. April 22, 2020. [Online] Available at: https://www.thenationalnews.com/arts-culture/art/why-maitha-demithan-hasn-t-yet-seen-her-striking-stayhome-artworks-on-sheikh-zayed-road-1.1009167 [Accessed January 6, 2022].

Bomb. (2020). 'Amani Al-Thuwaini and Andrea Hasler'. *Bomb Magazine*. May 19, 2020. [Online] Available at: https://bombmagazine.org/articles/amani-al-thuwaini-and-andrea-hasler/ [Accessed January 24, 2022].

Caravan. (n.d.). 'I Am'. [Online] Available at: https://www.oncaravan.org/i-am-exhibition [Accessed January 6, 2022].

Department of Culture and Tourism Abu Dhabi. (2020). 'Explore fabulous fashions of the past at Qasr al Hosn this December'. [Online] Available at: https://tcaabudhabi.ae/en/media.centre/news/explore.fabulous.fashions.of.the.past.at.qasr.al.hosn.this.december.aspx [Accessed January 7, 2022].

De Marchi, C. (2016). 'Mindful body: An introduction to body art and performance in the Gulf'. *Ibraaz*. 009, 14 April 2016. [Online] Available at: http://www.ibraaz.org/essays/146 [Accessed December 22, 2021].

Dib, F. and Hidayah, S. (2021). 'A pure moment of Arab pride'. *Fashion Trust Arabia*. November 4, 2021. [Online] Available at: https://fashiontrustarabia.com/a-pure-moment-of-arab-pride/ [Accessed January 6, 2022].

East, B. (2017). 'Emirati artist Maitha Demithan: "I feel that I am amidst a Renaissance"'. [Online] Available at: https://beneast.com/2017/08/19/emirati-artist-maitha-demithan-i-feel-that-i-am-amidst-a-renaissance/ [Accessed January 6, 2022].

Erskine-Loftus, P., Penziner-Hightower, V. and Al-Mulla, M. (eds.) (2019). *Representing the Nation: Heritage, Museums, National Narratives and Identity in the Gulf States*. London and New York: Routledge.

Esfandiari, S. (2021). 'Meet Nikki Meftah and Dima Abdul Kader, the founders of Emergeeast'. *Azeema*. July 6, 2021. [Online] Available at: https://www.azeemamag.com/stories/emergeast [Accessed January 4, 2022].

Exell, K. and Rico, T. (eds.) (2014). *Cultural Heritage in the Arabian Peninsula: Debates, Discourses and Practices*. London and New York: Routledge.

Faruque, N. (2021). 'The hand of history: Introducing a house of artisans, quite like no other...'. *Harper's Bazaar Arabia*, December 31, 2021. [Online] Available at: https://www.harpersbazaararabia.com/hbanews/house-of-artisans [Accessed January 7, 2022].

Kyba, M. (2021). '*Stories we tell ourselves*: Exhibition booklet'. [Online] Available at: https://foreman.ubishops.ca/stories-we-tell-ourselves/ [Accessed January 26, 2022].

Malluh, M. (2014). 'Food for Thought, Almuallaqat, 2014'. [Online] Available at: https://artbasel.com/catalog/artwork/20610/Maha-Malluh-Food-for-Thought-Almuallaqat [Accessed January 3, 2022].

Mathaf. (2020). 'Project Space 12: Bouthayna Al Muftah: Echoes'. [Online] Available at: https://www.mathaf.org.qa/en/ps-12-bouthayna-al-muftah [Accessed January 6, 2022].

Mollard, M. (2020). 'String of Pearls: The revitalisation of Muharraq takes visitors through Bahrain's pearling pathway and proves that the preservation of cultural heritage is compatible with bold architectural interventions'. *Architectural Review*, (1471), pp. 28–31.

Mousawi, A. (ed.) (2012). *Edge of Arabia: We Need to Talk*. Jeddah: Edge of Arabia.

Prager, L. (2015). 'Displaying origins: Heritage museums, cultural festivals, and national imageries in the UAE'. *Horizons in Humanities and Social Sciences*, 1(1), pp. 22–46.

Shehmir, A. (2021). 'Dana Awartani on preserving cultural identity, tradition and championing female empowerment through art'. *Harper's Bazaar Arabia*. December 8, 2021. [Online-Available at: https://www.harpersbazaararabia.com/culture/dana-awartani-interview [Accessed January 4, 2022].

Tedone, G. (2013). 'Maha Malluh: *Food for Thought II*, 2012'. [Online] Available at: https://www.tate.org.uk/art/artworks/malluh-food-for-thought-ii-t14014 [Accessed January 3, 2022].

Wakefield, S. (2020). *Cultural Heritage, Transnational Narratives and Museum Franchising in Abu Dhabi*. London and New York: Routledge.

2 Veiling and the Body

Hijab and Modest Dress

Perhaps no symbol of Muslim women has been as analyzed and contested as the *hijab*. The term can be used to refer generally to the concept of dressing modestly, but often is specifically linked to the veil, or head covering, worn by some Islamic women. In the Gulf states, the hijab is complemented by the *abaya*, which Noor Al-Qassimi (2010) describes as "a black, wide, loose garment with large wing-like sleeves and an opening in the front with no fastenings" (p. 46). She goes on to explain that "Donning the abaya constitutes a veiling practice and is an institutionalized form of national dress that is socio-legally implemented by the state" (p. 46).

According to Fereshteh Daftari (2006),

> In Western perception, the veil or chador has come to symbolize an asymmetry of power between men and women in the Islamic world. Inside that world, however, the veil confirms no single set of beliefs: *hijab* (the Islamic code of modest dress) may indeed be repressively enforced, but the wearing of the veil may also signify resistance to colonial and later secular powers, may be a relatively neutral matter of custom, may express religious faith, or may assert social status. In short the veil involves a spectrum of meanings that shift from one geographic, historical, and social context to another. It is no surprise that artists react to this array of signification in highly idiosyncratic ways.
>
> (p. 19)

The artists discussed in this chapter reference the hijab not just as a symbol of oppression but also as an index of female identity. Their work frequently moves beyond the literal representation or evocation

DOI: 10.4324/9781003197119-3

of the veil as a subject to address more broadly issues related to the female body and practices of seclusion and protection often found in patriarchal societies. They at times utilize metaphorical representation of veils and coverings to create works that are reflective and, at times, assertive in their approach to gender roles and identity.

Arwa Alneami

Never Never Land (2014), a photo and video installation by Saudi artist Arwa Alneami (born 1985), provides a surreptitious view of Saudi women at amusement parks in the provincial city of Abha, in the southwestern area of the country. In the parks, women's image and experience are tightly policed, with signs warning them to keep their abayas tightly wrapped in the rides and not to scream. Physical barriers keep men and women from glancing at one another and leather drapes attempt, not always successfully, to keep abayas in place, avoiding immodest exposure. Alneami's photos and videos, captured with a camera hidden in the folds of the artist's own abaya, both record the specific cultural constraints of Saudi society and offer a universal vision of human entertainment. Alneami views her work as part of a project of cultural criticism through humor, a means to criticize the status quo of Saudi society through the arts:

> Where censorship is widespread, satire, parody, and political humor are often the best or only means available to air opinions, voice dissent, or challenge government institutions or officials. Mockery can destroy mystique, break tensions, and disarm seemingly omnipotent, oppressive powers … This project uses the quality of humour to test the potential of art as a critical instrument for the analysis of social, political and cultural issues.
>
> (Alneami, n.d.)

The photos and videos, shot largely at night and juxtaposing the garish colors of the amusement parks with the black of the sky and of the women's abayas, are visually compelling. However, it is the travels of Alneami's work that may say the most about its potential success at opening a path to dialogue or criticism.

In the spring of 2016, works from *Never Never Land* were included in the exhibition *Spheres of Influence: Codes and Conduct Across Structural Landscapes* at the Mohsen Gallery in Tehran. Curated by American-based, Iranian-born Lila Nazemian, the exhibition was the first in Iran to feature works exclusively by Arab artists. Coming at a moment of political tension between Iran and several of the countries from which these artists hailed, the show's emphasis, according to the gallery, "is not political but social, intended to complicate and expand the views of an Iranian audience towards its neighbors and to challenge preconceived notions based on controlled pervasive narratives" (Mohsen Gallery, 2016). In this context, Alneami's work can be read as both illuminating and complicating narratives about the constraints placed on women in the Middle East. From a Western perspective, the restrictive dress codes upheld by both Saudi Arabia and Iran may appear homogeneous, in both cases requiring a level of covering that is viewed as oppressive. Yet, as art historian Christiane Gruber cautions, quoted in a review of the exhibition, this may be too simplistic a reading of the situation. For Gruber, works such as Alneami's may, rather than offering solidarity, present an opportunity for Iranians to uphold a critical view of Saudi:

> Many of the images – for example, of Saudi women driving bumper cars – nevertheless level an open critique of the Saudi regime for its infantilizing and control of women in various spheres of social and political life. These uncanny conjunctions of the holy and mundane, of the serious and ludic, yield tantalizing visual images. While these images may craft an 'East-East' visual conversation within Tehran, they nevertheless fit smoothly within a larger Iranian political discourse that, often rightly, lambasts Saudi Arabia's appalling treatment of its female citizens.
>
> (Geiger, 2016)

A 2018 exhibition in Wellington, New Zealand presented yet another opportunity for contrasting readings of Alneami's work. *Never Never Land* was exhibited at the City Gallery to mark the 125th year anniversary of women's suffrage in the country. New Zealand was the first country to give women the right to vote and to mark the anniversary the gallery opted to showcase work by a woman artist from the last country to give women the vote (women were first allowed to vote in Saudi Arabia in 2015). In selecting Alneami's work for this commemorative exhibition, the museum noted her increasing prominence within and outside the Kingdom and stated that "Her very presence as a contemporary artist challenges the restrictions her country places on female self-expression, as does her work" (City Gallery, 2018). In choosing to celebrate the work of a Saudi woman artist, City Gallery arguably provides an important international vehicle and venue for the exposure of an emerging talent. Yet, there is also the possibility that the cultural gaps between Saudi and New Zealand are too wide for the work to bridge; would viewers unfamiliar with the nuances of Saudi culture be able to fully appreciate the satire inherent in Alneami's photos and videos? In a thoughtful essay posted on the gallery's website, Anna Knox (2018), a New Zealander who has lived and worked in Saudi Arabia, questioned what gallery-goers would see and read in Alneami's images. Noting that the region from which Alneami comes, and where her photographs and videos were taken, has a vibrant tribal history in which cultural norms did not historically mandate veiling and separation of the sexes, Knox writes:

> But a New Zealand audience will likely focus on the foreground of burkhas and what they symbolise to us. On Alneami's website there is a photo of the artist, wearing neither western dress nor a burkha, but a niqab of gold, red, and blue, bedecked with gold circles and chains. What many people don't know is that the black body-and-face cover—now so fused with an understanding of Saudi—was part of the unification process. A country-wide dress-code for men and women buried local identities, replacing them with a national one. Consequently, regional and tribal dress have disappeared almost entirely in representations of Saudi. In Alneami's region, there are several powers at work in over-writing histories—including fundamentalism, modernisation, and nationalist frameworks. Against this background, her work becomes more nuanced and localised, and its narratives more interesting than an imagined endeavour to throw off the burkha and embrace Western freedom.

In its intersections and connections with audiences in locations as diverse as Tehran and Wellington, *Never Never Land* complicates its own narrative. The reactions of viewers are layered onto the already visually and contextually complicated and intentionally subversive images that Alneami has created, offering new avenues for interpretation and critique.

Waheeda Malullah

Bahraini artist Waheeda Malullah (born 1978) is known primarily for her work in photography and video, which she has exhibited both regionally and internationally since completing her undergraduate degree in 2002. Like Arwa Alneami, Malullah uses playfulness and satire to probe challenging questions about the gender roles, and constrictions placed on women, in her society. In early works, such as *Stopped Ball* (2003) an installation and series of reworked photographs, Malullah playfully inserted herself into traditionally male pastimes, such as football. Her use of the abaya as a marker of femininity in the work caused some viewers, including art critics Pat Binder and Gerhard Haupt, to question her intentions: "We asked her if this could mean that a breakaway from the traditional female role is problematic and maybe not so easy to realize." Malullah replied, somewhat vaguely, "I don't know ... sometimes yes, but we still try to smile!" (Binder & Haupt, 2004).

This exploration of the boundaries and experiences of Islamic women is foregrounded in later works, such as *A Villager's Day Out* (2008), a photographic series that was included as part of Bahrain's inaugural pavilion at the Venice Biennale in 2013. As with several other Gulf countries (notably the UAE in 2009 and Saudi Arabia in 2011), Bahrain prominently featured the work of women artists in its debut at the prestigious international event, a move that can be read as an overt attempt to quell concerns about gender discrimination in the region. Malullah stages photographs of a young woman fully covered by an enveloping, black abaya (the "villager" of the title) moving through the urban spaces of Manama variously appearing intimidated and at ease. The photographs work as a commentary not only on the culture shock experienced by Bahrainis at the rapid modernization of their society but also on the unease with which some Muslim women navigate public spaces and are visually framed by others. The inclusion of this work in an exhibition directed primarily toward a Western audience is not surprising given what Jessica Winegar (2015) notes as the preponderance of arts events "featuring female Middle Eastern artists and filmmakers whose work is presented and interpreted as showing, and therefore challenging, Middle Eastern gender inequalities seen as derived almost solely from Islam" (p. 668). Malullah's work can, through this lens, be read as questioning the presence of the veil as a means of excluding women fully from participation in contemporary society.

A 2016 retrospective of Malullah's work, *Little Voice*, held at the Bin Matar House Art Space in Bahrain, offered an opportunity to put the range of the artist's production in perspective and to observe the themes which developed in her art over time. Viewed across multiple works, the abaya becomes one of a series of markers of womanhood (hair is another prominent one) that shapes what curator Melissa Enders-Bhatia (2016) refers to as the "dualistic nature" of Malullah's work (p. 5). Explaining this dualism further, Enders-Bhatia (2016) writes that it is: "where the artist's appeal and success ultimately lies. A strong conceptual approach countered by spontaneity in execution. A playful innocence reverberating with deeper issues regarding the role of women, dress and religion in a traditional community" (p. 5). In the sometimes playful, often unexpected, juxtapositions of women's bodies with physical spaces and objects, Malullah invites us to examine our own expectations about women in the Gulf and women in hijab. The artist is open to multiple interpretations of her work, stating that "I feel an artwork is no longer mine once I have produced it, so I'm very open for the audience to see it from their perspective. Sometimes they love it. They think I am breaking rules!" (Enders-Bhatia, 2016, p. 9). By allowing the viewer to make the decision about whether Malullah is breaking rules, or gender expectations, with her work, the artist imparts an element of agency to that viewer, who may herself be a woman from the Gulf.

Maha Alasaker

In the 2015–2018 photographic series, *Women of Kuwait*, few of the women pictured wear the hijab. This is because the photographs, by Kuwaiti artist Maha Alasaker (born 1977), were taken in their subject's bedrooms, a private space in which women can drop their public persona and become themselves. As Hakim Bishara (2020) writes in *Hyperallergic*, the project is something of a double-edged sword:

> The series is the first to bring such a close and authentic glimpse into the personal environments of women in the country, presented by a Kuwaiti native. But it is also a *détournement* of an old orientalist trope in Western art: the depiction of Arab women as exotically enclosed in their harems, isolated from men and the outer world.

The ambivalence encoded in the subject and framing of the work emerges in the voices of the women photographed as well. The photographs, which Alasaker published as an artist's book in 2019, are accompanied by text from each sitter describing her thoughts on being a woman in Kuwait. The disparate descriptions range from positive, "Women in Kuwait has [sic] less appreciation & respect as I see it in my daily life," to negative, "It's not easy to be Kuwaiti women because of harsh judgmental society," but many capture a sense of ambivalence, "Being a Kuwaiti woman has been both a source of pride and a struggle my whole life" (Alasaker, n.d.). In an interview discussing the book's publication, Alasaker describes the process of creating the work as helping her to feel that she is part of collective societal struggle: "This last project made me think of *us* rather than *me*. I always felt that I am different from everyone else at home, but I realized that the struggles I go through are not mine alone" (Bishara, 2020).

Alasaker lived for several years in New York, first as a student at the International Center for Photography and then working on both artistic and commercial photographic projects. In 2017, following the election of Donald Trump as President and the Women's March in Washington, D.C., Alasaker's work was included in the street art project Resistance Is Female, in which posters featuring work by women artists and allies were placed on phone booths in New York as "a response to the Trump administration and aims to serve as a reminder to women and their allies of the need to keep fighting" (Cascone, 2017). The works by Alasaker were reproduced from her self-portrait series, *Belonging* (2016), in which she appears with her face partially covered – by her hands, or fabric, or sometimes just a shadow. Alasaker describes the work as

> about the feeling of being a woman, who struggles to fit in the society. I was addressing issues such as the double life that many people have in Kuwait. I was wearing abaya as a reference for covering and hiding. This work speaks about being different in your own skin.
>
> (Reconnecting Arts, 2017)

As part of the Resistance Is Female project, the works speak both to Alasaker's determination to represent herself and her lived experience and to the distances still to travel in achieving full recognition as a woman in Kuwaiti society.

Shurooq Amin

In a 2020 exhibit at the Contemporary Arts Platform in Kuwait, Kuwaiti artist Shurooq Amin (born 1967) deployed veils in an unusual way: by installing veiled mannequins around the exhibition space, to represent women who would not be allowed to attend the exhibition. In Amin's words,

> I wanted to tell such a woman that she can preserve the traditional identity within the framework of vital and renewed ideas that seeks to raise children, males in particular, on the basis of moral

values that make them men who are more accepting to the rights
of the opposite sex and being more tolerant to women.

(Elgayar, 2020)

The exhibition of Amin's paintings, titled *Like Russian Dolls, We
Nest in our Previous Selves*, was closed by the authorities one week
after its opening, with officials from the Ministries of the Interior
and of Information claiming that "her work was offensive to Kuwaiti
society" (Elgayar, 2020). Amin's large, bright canvases include depic-
tions of women in bikinis juxtaposed with men in traditional dress,
men and women cradling bottles of alcohol, figures locked in passion-
ate embraces and other representations that could be problematic in
a conservative Muslim culture. The artist explains that her work is
meant to address the hypocrisy in Kuwaiti culture, where an exter-
nal façade of religious decorum and respectability can hide a very
different set of personal behaviors. As she says, "I am a mirror of my
community, reflecting what I see ... I address the taboos Arabs refuse
to talk about, such as religious hypocrisy, adultery, homosexuality,
and alcoholism" (Elgayar, 2020). By focusing her attention on scantily
clad women while the men in her images wear the traditional Kuwaiti
dress, Amin both evokes an Orientalist style and questions the legitimacy of a patriarchal society in which actual veiled women may be
excluded from the public space of her exhibition, while Kuwaiti men
can visually consume both forbidden images and, she implies, the
forbidden women themselves. One painting in particular, *You Should
See Me in a Crown* (2019), echoes a common motif used throughout
the history of art to depict male hypocrisy and the problematics of
the male gaze: that of Susanna and the Elders. In Amin's painting, a
bikini-clad woman (wearing the crown of the title) sits in a window
frame, her body turned toward the viewer, but her eyes covered by
sunglasses to conceal her gaze. A man wearing the thobe and ghutra
bends toward her, hands outstretched as though cajoling or pleading
with the woman. In addition to the aversion suggested by the female
figure's turned body, the artist emphasizes her disinterest through the
scrawled word "leave" painted on the other side of the window the
woman is seated in. What appears to be a torn abaya also hangs in
that window frame, perhaps a suggestion that the modest garment is
no real deterrent to insistent male desire.

Amin maintains a sense of humor in the face of the difficult themes
she addresses in her work and despite attempts by the government to
curtail the public display of her art (the 2020 show was the second of
Amin's to be shut down; her 2012 exhibition *It's a Man's World* was

closed just hours after its opening). She is active on Instagram, where she promoted a series of works created in part as a response to the 2020 exhibition closure titled *They Wanted Camels, I Gave Them Camels.* The paintings feature figures from the works in the *Like Russian Dolls* show, positioned on images of camel skulls. The artist is selling the works as NFT's, explaining on her website that

> This second-time censorship has fueled Amin to further expose hypocrisy in the Muslim world. And as such, Amin has turned to the world of NFTs as a platform for freedom of expression, using NFT art as a utility for freedom, getting her message across universally without fear of oppression or censorship.
>
> (Amin, 2021)

Perhaps new technologies and market strategies will afford new venues for the display of works that are difficult to publicly exhibit in museums and galleries in Kuwait itself.

Manal Al Dowayan

The prolific Saudi artist Manal Al Dowayan (born 1973) works in a variety of media including sculpture, photography, video and sound. She is perhaps best known for her large-scale, participatory installations such as *Suspended Together* (2011; discussed in the introduction to this volume) and *Esmi-My Name* (2012), which were produced as "the result of workshops offering channels for thousands of women in the Kingdom to address unjust social customs" (Al Dowayan, n.d.). In the context of a chapter discussing artists' use of the hijab in their work, however, Al Dowayan's relatively early photographic series, *I Am* (2005) provides a critical reference point for women artist's engagement with this topic. In this series, Al Dowayan presents black and white portraits of Saudi women who maintained professional careers as educators, engineers, artists and others. In Al Dowayan's words:

> The collection of black and white photographs hosts a variety of Saudi Arabian women who perform everyday roles in Saudi society. At the same time, each photograph has a piece of traditional jewelry placed in an obstructive and unnatural way, questioning cultural traditions that prevent Saudi women from expanding their societal roles. *I Am* was produced in 2005 when less than 3% of Saudi Arabian women were formally employed. Today [2017] that number has risen to 16%. Regardless of the modest rise

in numbers, the main challenges have not changed from when I took these photographs. Politicians and religious figures in Saudi Arabia have, for years, hijacked the dialogue on women's rights. They have turned women's right to work in a public sphere into an issue that threatens Saudi identity, the structures of family, and the religious principles that underpin Muslim society.

(Al Dowayan, n.d.)

The women in the photographs are covered by hijab and/or the heritage jewelry referenced by Al Dowayan, in addition to wearing or holding an object symbolizing their jobs. The images thus layer markers of the multiple, and sometimes conflicting, roles of women in contemporary Saudi society; the hijab does not merely conceal but can also serve as a backdrop for more critical indicators of status and responsibility.

Afra Al Dhaheri

Mona Hatoum created *Keffieh* (1993–1999) by weaving women's hair into the form of the typical checked headscarf worn by many Palestinian and other Arab men. Homi Bhabha (2006) interpreted *Keffieh* as a symbol of female resistance:

One could suggest that the living female hair woven into this garment, so widely worn in regions where many women veil their heads outdoors, extends the public domain to include the rights of women and thus introduces the representation of 'difference' as something other than a homogenizing principle of universal equality.

(p. 34)

Emirati artist Afra Al Dhareri (born 1988) also uses hair as a medium and metaphor, in works such as *Fil Al Shaar* (2020) and *One at a Time* (2020), both included in the artist's solo exhibition *Split Ends* held at Green Art Gallery in Dubai in 2021. As Munira Al Sayegh (2021) writes in her description of the exhibition,

The cultural dichotomies of hair are framed throughout the exhibition simultaneously in both the understandings of hair through the domains of the public and private ... The juxtaposition of the organic and inorganic, embody both strength and vulnerability. Rope mimics the delicate language of hair but also evokes processes of tying down, taming, and tidying.

This emphasis on taming and tidying, as well as on the liminal properties of hair, is what connects Al Dhaheri's work to the concepts of modesty and hijab addressed in this chapter. In the sculptural installation *Fil Al Shaar*, cords of rope hang from the ceiling of the gallery, impeding the viewer's movement through the space. The ropes in this respect act as a veil, dividing and obscuring a part of the gallery space. Yet these ropes also offer the possibility of passage, unlike a woman's hijab, in that there is nothing preventing the viewer from walking through them. In an artist's talk, Al Dhaheri (2022) explained that leaving that choice to the viewer was important to her as a component of the work, offering a dichotomous presentation of the rope curtain as either hiding or revealing, depending on the viewer's choices and actions. In this way, the piece functions as a metaphor for the use of the veil to both conceal and in some respects to liberate, by allowing women to pass freely in public without concerns about immodesty or unwanted attention.

Boushra Almutawakel

Although this book focuses on GCC countries and thus does not include substantial analysis of women artists from Yemen (which, due to the ongoing war in the country, also struggles to maintain any substantial contemporary art scene) any discussion of Gulf artists whose work deals with veils and veiling would be incomplete without inclusion of the Yemeni photographer Boushra Almutawakel (born 1969). Almutawakel's series *Hijab* (ongoing since 2001) includes a variety of images, the best known of which is likely the set titled *Mother, Daughter, Doll* (2012), which has been exhibited internationally and is in the collection of the British Museum. In the nine photographs that comprise this work, Almutawakel poses with her daughter on her lap, the child holds a doll in her arms. As the images progress from left to right, the three figures become progressively more covered in black hijab, abaya, niqab and gloves until, in the last image, they disappear into the black backdrop. While the work has been analyzed and interpreted by critics from around the world, in response to a question of who she made the work for, Almutawakel stated that

> I made it first and foremost for a Yemeni audience. I was asking my society many things, like: To what extent will we cover our women. What is enough? The covering is about the literal covering, but also about so much more that is symptomatic of the state and status of women in our culture.
>
> (Porter, 2015; p. 215)

Almutawakel explained that she wanted the work to be able to be displayed in Yemen and that she was not criticizing the wearing of the hijab, per se, but more the extremes to which conservative religious Yemenis might push women to cover themselves. Speaking of the project as a whole, Almutawakel acknowledged the complexities of working with the veil as an artistic subject, particularly when her images would be seen by both Middle Eastern and Western audiences:

> I found the veil to be an intriguing, complex, multilayered topic. In this ongoing project on the hijab/veil I want to explore the many faces and facets of the veil based on my own personal experiences and observations: the convenience, freedom, strength, power, liberation, limitations, danger, humor, irony, variety, cultural, social, and religious aspects, as well as the beauty, mystery, and protection. The hijab/veil as a form of self-expression; the veil as not solely an Arab Middle Eastern phenomenon, the trends, the history and politics of the hijab/veil, as well as differing interpretations, and the fear in regards to the hijab/veil. I also want to be careful not to fuel the stereotypical widespread negative images most commonly portrayed about the hijab/veil in the Western media, especially the notion that most, or all women who wear the hijab/veil, are weak, oppressed, ignorant, and backwards. Furthermore, I hope to challenge and look at both Western and Middle Eastern stereotypes, fears, and ideas regarding the veil.
>
> (Muslima, n.d.)

In her ongoing work with this potent and problematic symbol, Almutawakel raises critical questions about the positioning and interpretation of the veil as a metaphor for women's lives in the Middle East.

Transcending the Limits

In the fall of 2019, the College of Arts and Creative Enterprises at Zayed University in the United Arab Emirates presented an exhibition of BFA Visual Arts students' work titled *Transcending Limits of Hope, Aspiration and Fear*. Many of the works in that exhibition, which was on view at Alserkal Avenue in Dubai, addressed issues of gender, identity and the female body. Hessa Al Fahim's triptych *A Girl Is Like a White Sheet* (2019) is a large-scale, mixed-media and oil on canvas work that depicts three women standing facing the viewer but covered by stained, white sheets, almost as if in a shroud. These oil paintings are themselves covered by a thin netting on which the artist made body prints in black ink, contributing to the staining effect. The title of the work reflects an Arabic saying that translates to "a girl is like a white sheet," which the artist describes as "insinuating that a woman's mistakes and flaws are easily visible [and] her decisions would immensely affect her family and reputation" (Hurley & Willems, 2019; p. 5). The worry about a stain on a woman's reputation leads to the overprotectiveness and limitations placed on many Arab women, a kind of metaphorical veiling or wrapping that is expressed visually by the sheet and netting in Al Fahim's work.

Similarly, Amira Albastaki's *The Safe Haven of Women* (2019) also addresses the issue of the oppression of women through a mixed-media sculptural installation. Albastaki has created a non-functional bedroom setting of bed, chair and pillow wrapped in blood-red, yarn-wrapped steel wires to create a sense of unease and discomfort. She explains that the baseless bed and dysfunctional chair "evoke anxiety and discomfort" and "represent the uncomfortable and suffocating life which society forces on women in the name of protection" (Hurley & Willems, 2019; p. 9). Albastaki's work, like Al Fahim's, addresses the negative consequences of an overprotective, leading to

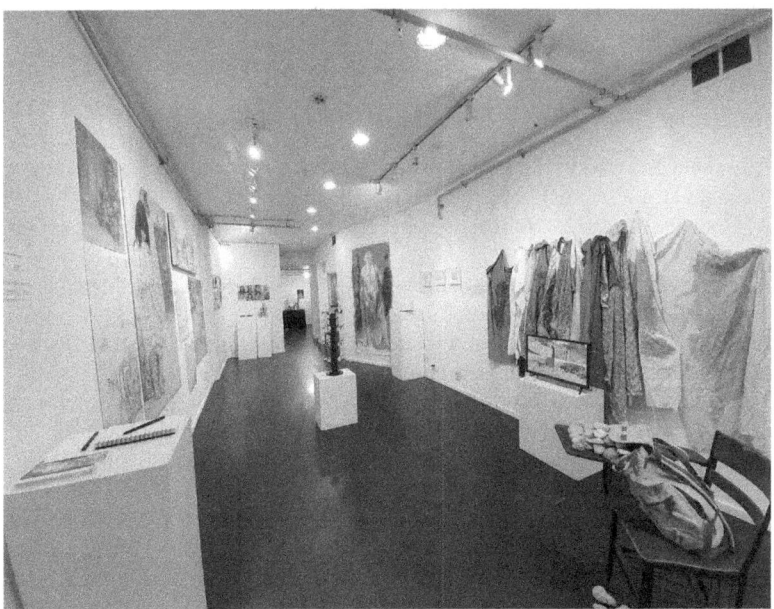

Figure 2.1 Installation view of *Transcending the Limits* on display in Philadelphia. Photograph by the author.

oppressive, family structure and patriarchal culture that can contribute to feelings of invisibility and futility on the part of women, particularly young women like these artists.

Hassana Arif, in her work *Between Our Lines* (2019), "reject[s] the idea that we are supposed to conform to a specific feminine ideal, or that all women should adhere to one" (Hurley & Willems, 2019; p. 39). Arif's set of screen prints on paper are unique identity markers that the artist has created by rendering an identification photograph (for example, from a passport) into a series of abstract lines that are reminiscent of a fingerprint. These forms are surrounded by text of quotations from the woman represented, all of whom the artist interviewed for the project. The work presents female identity in a wholly unique and novel way, while still adhering to cultural restrictions on photographing and representing images of women, particularly in a public venue such as an art exhibit. In this regard, the artist finds a new mode of representation that both nods to the practice of veiling or covering but also allows female self-expression to come to the foreground. Following its run in Dubai, a selection of works from the exhibition were on view in 2020 in the United States in Philadelphia, Chicago and at the University of North Alabama, allowing a wider audience to appreciate the social, cultural and personal investigations of these emerging Emirati women artists.

References

Alasaker, M. (n.d.). 'Artist's website'. [Online] Available at: https://www.mahaalasaker.com/ [Accessed January 13, 2022].

Al Dhaheri, A. (2022). 'Split ends'. *College Art Association Annual Conference*. Virtual, February 16–19.

Al Dowayan, M. (n.d.). 'Artist's website'. [Online] Available at: https://www.manaldowayan.com [Accessed January 10, 2022].

Alneami, A. (n.d.). 'Artist's website'. [Online] Available at: http://www.arwaalneami.com/ [Accessed January 10, 2022].

Al Sayegh, M. (2021). 'Split ends: Afra Al Dhaheri'. [Online] Available at: https://www.gagallery.com/exhibitions/split-ends [Accessed May 9, 2022].

Amin, S. (2021). 'About'. [Online] Available at: https://www.shurooqamin.com/about [Accessed January 24, 2022].

Bhabha, H. (2006). 'Another country'. In Daftari, F. ed. *Without Boundary: Seventeen Ways of Looking*. New York: Museum of Modern Art, pp. 30–35.

Binder, P. and Haupt, G. (2004). 'Waheeda Malullah'. *Nafas*. June 2004. [Online] Available at: https://universes.art/en/nafas/articles/2004/waheeda-malullah [Accessed January 13, 2022].

Bishara, H. (2020). 'A Kuwaiti artist photographs women in the intimate sanctuary of their bedrooms'. *Hyperallergic*. February 28, 2020. [Online]

Available at: https://hyperallergic.com/535467/maha-alasaker-women-in-kuwait/ [Accessed January 13, 2022].

Cascone, S. (2017). 'Proclaiming "resistance is female," guerrilla artists commandeer NYC phone booths'. *Artnews*. April 3, 2017. [Online] Available at: https://news.artnet.com/art-world/resistance-female-guerrilla-art-overruns-new-york-phone-booths-912416 [Accessed January 13, 2022].

City Gallery. (2018). 'Arwa Alneami: Never Never Land'. [Online] Available at: https://citygallery.org.nz/exhibitions/arwa-alneami-never-never-land/ [Accessed January 10, 2022].

Daftari, F. (2006). 'Islamic or not'. In Daftari, F. ed. *Without Boundary: Seventeen Ways of Looking*. New York: Museum of Modern Art, pp. 10–27.

Elgayar, A. (2020). 'Kuwait shuts down an art exhibit. Is the "most open" Gulf society closing?' *Al-Fanar Media*. February 25, 2020. [Online] Available at: https://www.al-fanarmedia.org/2020/02/kuwait-shuts-down-an-art-exhibit-is-the-most-open-gulf-society-closing/ [Accessed January 24, 2022].

Enders-Bhatia, M. ed. (2016). 'Waheeda Malullah: *Little Voice*'. Bahrain: Sheikh Ebrahim bin Mohammed Al-Khalifa Center for Cultural Research. [Online] Available at: https://shaikhebrahimcenter.org/en/event/waheeda-malullahs-little-voice/ [Accessed January 13, 2022].

Geiger, D. (2016). 'Why Iran's first contemporary Arab art exhibit was important'. *Vice*. June 7, 2016. [Online] Available at: https://www.vice.com/en/article/mvkjj8/why-irans-first-contemporary-arab-art-exhibit-was-important [Accessed January 10, 2022].

Hurley, Z. and Willems, W. (2019). *Transcending Limits of Hope, Aspiration and Fear*. Dubai and Abu Dhabi: Zayed University.

Knox, A. (2018). 'Every house has its own story'. [Online] Available at: https://citygallery.org.nz/blog/every-house-has-its-own-story/ [Accessed January 10, 2022].

Mohsen Gallery. (2016). 'Spheres of influence'. [Online] Available at: https://mohsen.gallery/exhibitions/spheres-of-influence/ [Accessed January 10, 2022].

Muslima. (n.d.). 'The hijab/veil series: Boushra Almutawakel, Yemen'. [Online] Available at: http://muslima.globalfundforwomen.org/content/hijab-veil-series [Accessed January 25, 2022].

Porter, V. (2015). 'Histories of the present: The changing worlds of Middle Eastern artists'. In Keshmirshekan, H. ed. *Contemporary Art from the Middle East: Regional Interactions with Global Art Discourses*. London: I.B. Tauris, pp. 203–219.

Reconnecting Arts. (2017). 'Kuwaiti photographer Maha Alasaker and her thoughts on identity and belonging'. [Online] Available at: https://reconnectingarts.com/2017/03/01/maha-alasaker-and-her-thoughts-on-identity-and-belonging/ [Accessed January 13, 2022].

Winegar, J. (2008). 'The humanity game: Art, Islam, and the war on terror'. *Anthropological Quarterly*, 81(3), pp. 651–681. Available at: https://www.jstor.org/stable/2548828 [Accessed January 10, 2022].

3 Modernization and Urban Growth

Modernization and Urban Development

The rapid development of the Gulf states after the discovery of oil is one of the key hallmarks of the region's cultural, economic and political identity (Elsheshtawy, 2011; Molotch & Ponzini, 2019). The gleaming skyscrapers rising seemingly overnight from desert sands represent one facet of this development; changes to social norms and expectations of women, at least as officially pronounced, form another strand of the modernization projects beloved in the region (Tripp, 2019). The artists discussed in this chapter find inspiration in the changing physical, cultural and economic landscapes of the Gulf. Their works address issues ranging from the pervasive construction sites throughout cities such as Dubai, Doha and Riyadh to the marginalization of heritage, to the advent of an oil economy and the realities of entering a post-oil economic strategy in the region. They work in a variety of media, similar to the varied architectural forms that populate Gulf cities. The chapter concludes with a brief analysis of the impact of cultural organizations as drivers of urban development and tourism in the Gulf as the countries in this region reshape their visions of a twenty-first-century future.

Zeinab Al Hashemi

Emirati artist Zeinab Al Hashemi (born 1985) is perhaps best known for her three-dimensional works; however, her photographic series *Urban Phantasmagoria* (2013–2016) also reflects several themes and concepts that are critical to her practice. The works in the series are created from composite satellite photos of Dubai and Abu Dhabi and incorporate Al Hashemi's fascination with patterns, mapping and the representation of space and time (Al Hashemi, n.d.). For

DOI: 10.4324/9781003197119-4

the photographs in *Urban Phantasmagoria* Al Hashemi focused on mapping and urban design as concepts underpinning the images. The photographs have a kaleidoscopic quality and this distortion some-times completely abstracts the landscape, leaving little reference for the viewer other than color and pattern. In other images, however, signal landmarks such as the Burj Al Arab or Burj Khalifa form a repetitive hallmark that both grounds the viewer in space and time while expanding our horizons through the destabilizing repetition. Al Hashemi is interested in the way the cities of Dubai and Abu Dhabi were put together, seeing them as "well designed rather than organic" (Artist interview, 2018). Her own highly choreographed and impecca-bly rendered photographs reflect that intentional design not only in their subject but in their style.

Al Hashemi describes one of the main ideas behind *Urban Phantasmagoria* as showing "not what is, but rather what could be" (Artist interview, 2018). Photography has since its earliest days been associated with both realism and manipulation and is thus a fitting medium for explorations and documentations of change in space, time and landscape. *Urban Phantasmagoria* also considers the relationship between manmade and natural environments, and the tensions that can exist between these two states. The photographs in the series fea-ture both urban and desert landscapes and several show the sometimes uneasy balance between the two that is visible in the UAE. Sand dunes encroach on the edges of suburban housing tracts while vast resort complexes shape the ebb and flow of the Arabian Gulf. The rapid pace and large scale of development in the UAE have frequently been noted as placing the manmade in tension with the natural, or perhaps with the traditional, and Al Hashemi's photographs, with their disorienting appearance, nod to that tension.

One of Al Hashemi's large-scale projects, *Metamorphic* (2017), was designed for the exhibition *Co-Lab: Contemporary Art and Savoir-faire*, one of the inaugural exhibitions of the Louvre Abu Dhabi. This sculptural installation, produced in conjunction with the French stained-glass factory Verrerie Saint-Just, at first glance seems to bear no relationship to the photographs of *Urban Phantasmagoria*. However, Al Hashemi sees *Metamorphic* as a "continuation" of that earlier work as the new sculpture also references mapping, landscape and the relationship between the natural and manmade, albeit in a more oblique way than the photographs (Artist interview, 2018). The sculpture combines stained glass and metal mesh, with squares of glass arranged on the metal in ways that both highlight the inher-ent patterns in the mesh and also create new ones. The colors of the glass reflect elements in the topography of Saadiyat Island, where the Louvre Abu Dhabi is located, specifically the sand and water of and around the island. The mesh itself is the rebar (or reinforcing steel) ubiquitous in construction projects throughout the UAE, thus providing the manmade juxtaposition to the earthly elements reflected by the stained glass (Seaman, 2018). In this work, Al Hashemi captures the multifaceted reality of Gulf construction projects as they both displace and create, shaping the region's landscape in ways that will be felt for decades to come.

Radhika Khimji

Curator Aisha Stoby (2009) writes,

> In a world which has become increasingly nationally ambiguous and more rapidly in flux than ever before, many of [Radhika] Khimji's pieces deal with themes of contemporary Orientalism and globalisation... She perceives the modernization of countries like Oman and other nations in the Gulf region occurring at such a rapid speed that their respective past histories are in danger of becoming lost and fragmented.

Khimji (born 1979) is an Omani artist whose works range from large-scale installations to mixed-media canvases. Her works explore shifting territories of both bodies and physical spaces; indeed, her early works featured amorphous forms the artist referred to as

> shifters ... cut out shapes performing different gestures in space. They reference a frozen body caught in a state of movement, and are informed by my research into post-colonial theory and the creation of an identity as a subject and an other. I made them to be out of context, as slightly alien and not fully formed, bodies in stasis and without ground.
>
> (Khimji, n.d.)

Of particular interest in the context of modernization, however, are the installation works that Khimji created first in 2010 at the Barka Fort in Oman and then for the 2016 Marrakech Biennale. *Safe Landings* (2010) was Khimji's first solo show in Oman and the installation at Barka Fort featured the cut-out, painted forms of her "shifters" combined with parachutes draped over the walls of the old fort. For Khimji, the liminality and layered history of the space was an important component of a work in which she wanted to use a heritage site to question categorizations and constructions of identity. In an interview, Khimji described the relevance of the site to her work:

> Barka Fort is a really special site, and I have been thinking for some time about heritage spaces in Oman and what they mean today. Barka was once a strategic trade capital in the late 18th century. In an effort to prevent harassment in Omani waters, the ruling Sultan handed over the use of Muscat's port to the Persians and moved to the town of Barka. Ultimately, as major trade routes were redirected to pass through this town, the move enabled the Omanis to regain full control of Muscat. By changing trade routes, the Omanis were thus able to preserve their position with dignity and strength. The displacement of the port from one place to another, for a short period of time, created a sense of hovering between two places. I found this narrative really empowering when I read it and thought it was a different take on displacement as the interim period did not disorientate the people's identity.
>
> (Binder & Haupt, 2010)

The idea of connections between physical spaces and cultural identity is one that resonates strongly within the Gulf region, where the rapid destruction of old sites during the rush to modernization has left many regretting the loss of important physical markers of community identity.

In 2016, Khimji was included in the Marrakech Biennale where she showed a work similar in form to *Safe Landings*. In Marrakech, she installed parachutes in two locations in a work titled *Stay Safe* (2016). The parachutes were trapped in their surroundings on the walls of an old palace and a mosque; draped over the stone and with ropes dangling uselessly around them they conveyed little of the safety alluded to in the work's title. Writing about the work in *Artforum*, Myrna Ayad (2016) describes its irony:

> There is something tragic about this abandoned, neglected parachute. Thrown across a wall of the sixteenth-century El Badi Palace, this white symbol of a descent here looks almost accidental. And yet the piece also suggests an arrival while hinting at shelter or escape. Isn't a parachute meant to land in a safe spot? White

is the shroud that covers the dead; how helpless we appear in the face of conflicts that necessitate such wrappings.

The parachutes in Khimji's work become reflections of the uncertainties of physical space, uncertainties which are writ large in the historical and contemporary conditions of the Middle East. These uncertainties are reflected in the process of modernization as much as in the territorial and religious conflicts that have torn through the region and Khimji's work offers a nuanced reminder of their ongoing presence.

Monira Al Qadiri

Born in Senegal, raised in Kuwait, educated in Japan and currently resident in Berlin, Kuwaiti artist Monira Al Qadiri (born 1983) brings a global and multi-disciplinary perspective to her work as an artist in sculpture, video and mixed-media installations. She earned a Ph.D. in 2010, with research that focused on the aesthetics of sadness in the Middle East, and that interest informs her artistic exploration of the petro-culture of the Gulf and its past, present and future impacts on society and the environment. Her sculptural practice includes several works that use drill bits and other elements of oil drilling equipment as the basis for iridescent, seemingly abstract forms that, with their glossy, colored surfaces, distract from the utilitarian nature of the objects they are constructed from. These works have an affinity with pop art in their smooth surfaces and candy-like colors; they perhaps also share a language of cultural critique in which the foundations of a consumerist society quite literally fueled by petroleum are called into question. One of her early works in this vein, *Alien Technology* (2014), was produced as a public sculpture in Dubai, positioned in a heritage area along the waterfront (other iterations of the work were shown subsequently in Minneapolis and Venice). A large-scale, biomorphic shape rises from the sand; this object is a drill used in oil extraction, but its form is reminiscent of marine life. The intersections between oil and sea are intentional, given the importance of pearling as an industry in Kuwait and other Gulf countries prior to the discovery of oil. Al Qadiri's grandfather was a singer on the pearling dhows and she views these sculptures as a sort of self-portrait, as an excavation of her own past as well as her country's:

> Actually the second work about oil that I made, *Alien Technology*,
> was this giant public sculpture of an oil drill in Dubai, placed next

to pearl-diving boats. It's in a heritage village and the pearl-diving boats are actually these fake ones made for touristic consumption. So I made this public sculpture of a drill there. I felt that the drill was a self-portrait. It's a representation of who I am, placed next to the boat, which is my grandfather.

(Alsaden, 2021)

Al Qadiri's 2018 video work, *Diver*, explores the transition from pre-oil Kuwait to the current petro-state while also bringing the issue of gender roles into the frame. The video shows a group of women, clad in iridescent body suits, performing a synchronized swimming routine in dark water. The soundtrack is a recording from the 1960s of pearl-diving songs. Al Qadiri describes her vision of the work:

I just imagined the scene of synchronised swimming in the ocean at night so that the water would look like oil, and that these swimmers would be dressed in dichroic colour bodysuits and they would be choreographed to the songs of the pearl divers.

(Alsaden, 2021)

The connection between pearling and oil is achieved through the play of color and light; the black of the water, the iridescence of the women's suits, both evoke the colors of an oil slick or the black surface of a pool of oil as well as the blackness of water at night and the changeable colors of the oyster and its pearl. That the swimmers are women plays with the gendered history of pearling, in which the divers and boat crews were all male. Al Qadiri calls into question constructions of history and identity:

The images of pearl-diving and boats and the music is always promoted in a way that they represent our history and identity. But then our lives in this oil economy are completely and utterly detached from that world. So there is this kind of cognitive dissonance there about self-identity. In this work, I also wanted to play a lot on the idea of gender, because the world of pearl-diving is male-dominated.

(Alsaden, 2021)

Oil, pearling, gender roles, modernity and personal and collective identity are among the themes explored by the artist in her evolving body of work.

Hind Mezaina

Emirati photographer Hind Mezaina (born 1971) explores issues of collective memory, heritage and the media representation of Dubai in her work, which documents the changing landscape of the city and its environs, focusing on the unnoticed interstices of the modern urban environment. In *Dubai Hills* (2017), the artist captures images of the piles of earth, rock and sand that are ubiquitous in Dubai, a city under constant construction and reconstruction. As Mezaina describes,

> Dubai is subjected to ongoing construction. This constant change can be seen in the heaps of sand that dot the city; the stones and bricks are piled everywhere – especially around construction sites. I see these heaps every day, wherever I am driving in the city. Over time, I'm come to regard them as our very own hills.
>
> (Mezaina, n.d.)

The photographs are arranged in such a way that at first glance they could appear to be mountain or desert landscapes; it is only on closer inspection that the viewer understands these "hills" to be manmade, refuse from the ongoing project of urbanization and growth.

In 2021, Mezaina presented a solo show, *Wonder Land*, at Tashkeel Studio and Gallery in Dubai. The show was the culminating product of the artist's participation in Tashkeel's Critical Practice Program, an artist mentorship program that has been ongoing since 2014. Mezaina produced the works in *Wonder Land* during the COVID-19 lockdown in Dubai, when she was unable to travel internationally and focused her attention on the changes the pandemic environment created in the familiar city, resulting in images in which

> her intentional gaze brings to the foreground nuances and hitherto unnoticed elements of the urban fabric, indicative of an environment in flux; from the abandoned remnants of constant progress to the reclamatory force of nature over human endeavour. Amid the unnerving emptiness, cosmetic distractions and constructed artifices stand hollow like an abandoned fairground, devoid of meaning as the once unrelenting momentum of ambition slows to a halt.
>
> (Tashkeel, 2021)

The photographs capture the leftover spaces vacated during the pandemic, for example, blank billboards towering above the highways, as well as the insistent reassertion of the natural world into urban spaces left untended during lockdown. Mezaina describes the experience of creating the work as a transition from driving (the ubiquitous mode of transportation in Dubai) to walking in a newly quietened city:

> It started off with long drives that I took in Dubai when most places were closed in the first few months of the pandemic. It was a way to get some relief from staying at home and for some needed change of scenery. Seeing parts of the city dotted with blank billboards grabbed my attention, and to me they symbolized 2020. I wanted to get closer to these billboards to photograph, and I also incorporated walking in different parts of Dubai to enjoy a slower pace of experiencing the city and also noticing things that one wouldn't see whilst driving.

> (Khaleejesque, 2021)

Mezaina's photographs offer an alternative space for reflection on the fast-paced development of Dubai, by documenting an enforced pause and its aftereffects, a blip in the unrelenting path of modernization that has become the city's hallmark.

Cultural Sector

The development of the cultural sector in Gulf countries is a part of the modernization process, linked to the region's drive to diversify revenue streams in preparation for a post-oil economy. The countries of the Gulf, particularly Bahrain, Qatar, Saudi Arabia and the UAE, are investing heavily in projects in the art and design sectors, both to boost tourism and to entice local and international investments from creative sector companies. In many cases, women are playing leading roles in these projects and the case studies discussed below offer a glimpse of the intersections between art, gender and urban development in the Gulf.

Art Jameel

Since its founding in 2003, Art Jameel has been one of the principal drivers of a renewed interest in Islamic art and design, including both traditional and contemporary practices, in the Middle East and beyond. Launched under the umbrella of the Saudi philanthropic organization Community Jameel, Art Jameel quickly established itself

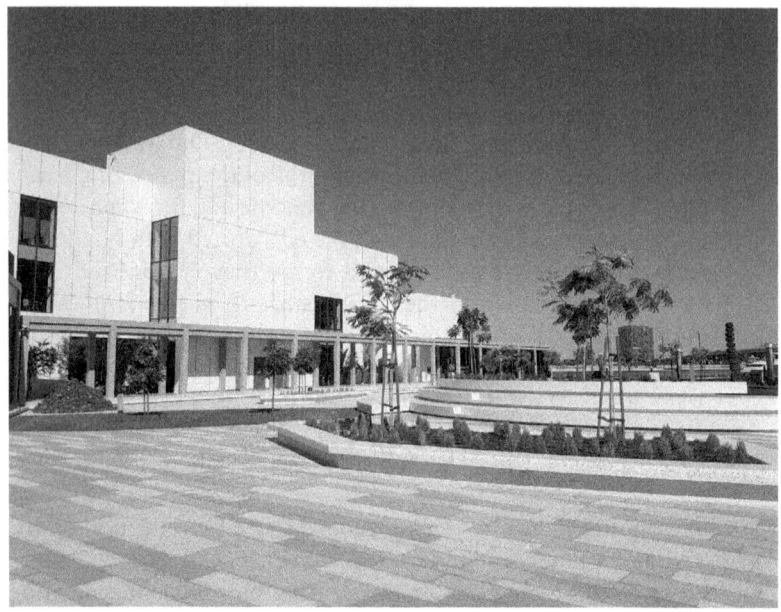

Figure 3.1 Art Jameel's Dubai campus on the shores of Dubai Creek. Photograph by the author.

as a powerful force in the art world, with its support of the renovation of the Victoria and Albert Museum's Islamic gallery in 2003, the establishment of the Jameel House of Traditional Arts in Cairo in 2009 and the establishment of the Jameel Prize for contemporary art in the Islamic tradition (in partnership with the V&A) in the same year (Art Jameel, 2022).

In 2016, Antonia Carver was appointed as Director of Art Jameel. Formerly on the staff of *Bidoun* magazine and the director of Art Dubai from 2010 until her move to Art Jameel, Carver is an active force in the development of a contemporary arts scene in the Gulf. Her work at Art Jameel has focused on opening two major centers for contemporary art in the region: Jameel Arts Centre in Dubai (opened 2018) and Hayy Jameel in Jeddah (opened 2021). Both centers are focused on bringing serious, cutting-edge contemporary art exhibitions and educational programming to the region, on a scale and of an international caliber not seen in previous projects. Carver's background in writing and publishing about art in the Middle East, combined with her in-depth knowledge of the art market and galleries in the region, is instrumental in orchestrating exhibits and events that demonstrate a commitment to intellectual rigor while offering opportunities for sustained critical engagement with local communities. The opening exhibition at Jameel Arts Centre, *Crude*, curated by Murtaza Vali (2018), took aim directly at the role that discovery of oil and its exportation played in the "petromodernity" of the Middle East, immediately situating the gallery as a space for dialogue around the complicated aftereffects of the regional growth spurred by oil. As Vali writes,

> By beginning to unearth the repressed histories of colonialism and imperialism that accompanied Western endeavours to secure oil, these works allow us to trace the lingering impacts of these processes in the present. At the same time, 'Crude' seeks to initiate a long-overdue and much-needed regional conversation around oil and the deleterious effects—social and cultural, and environmental—of our petrodepence.
>
> (p. 81)

The Jameel Arts Centre is situated in a new development on Dubai Creek, in an area central to the emirate's ongoing urban development and touristic strategies. To immediately engage with the complex and problematic history of the sources of the wealth that makes such development possible suggests that the Jameel Arts Centre may be able to foster a new level of dialogue around future directions for Gulf states, using contemporary art as a catalyst for critical conversations. If Hayy Jameel can foster similar conversations and critical investigations in Saudi Arabia, the potential for interchange and engagement both within the region and beyond is significant.

Alserkal Avenue

On the other side of the city from Jameel Arts Centre, Dubai's Alserkal Avenue has been growing as an arts district since 2008, when the first intrepid galleries opened spaces in warehouse buildings in the Al Quoz neighborhood. As I have discussed elsewhere (DeTurk, 2020), Alserkal Avenue has grown largely through the importation of galleries from outside the UAE (e.g., Leila Heller, Custot, Jean-Paul Najar) and the number of Emirati and Gulf artists featured in their rosters is unfortunately small. However, since around 2019, Executive Director of Alserkal Vilma Jurkute seems to be steering the organization in a direction that foregrounds local talent and engages the local arts community in important ways. Among these is the launch of the Alserkal

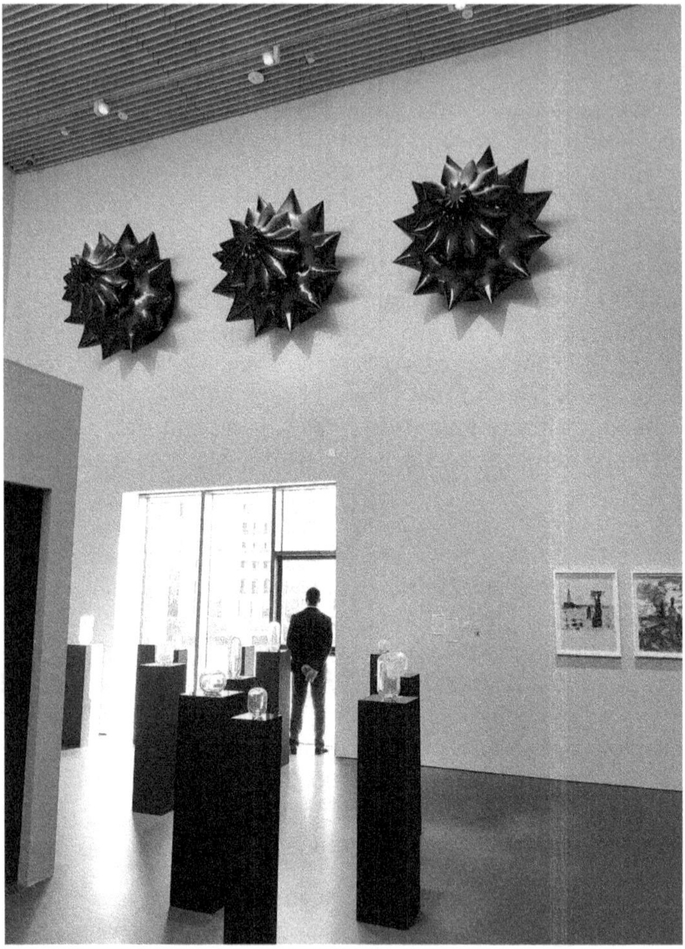

Figure 3.2 Installation view of the *Crude* exhibit at Jameel Art Centre with a sculpture by Monira Al Qadiri on the wall. Photograph by the author.

Arts Foundation, which supports artist projects, awards research grants, offers residencies and sponsors cultural programs. Early projects and participants included Moza Almatrooshi, an Emirati conceptual artist who staged her performance piece, *The Alphabetics of the Barista* (2021), at Alserkal Avenue. The event was noteworthy not only for its featuring of an Emirati woman artist working in performance,

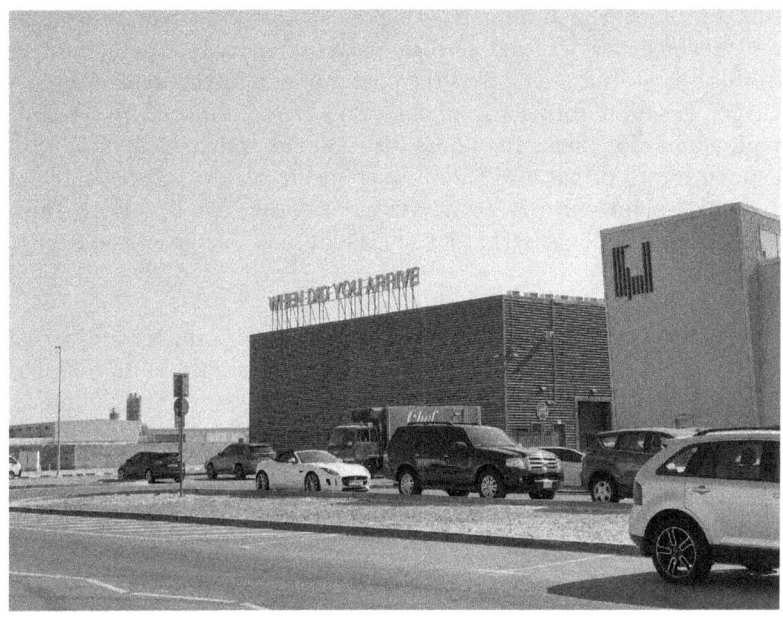

Figure 3.3 The entrance to Alserkal Avenue with a section of Mary Ellen
Carroll's sculptural installation *The Circle Game* (2016). Photograph
by the author.

still a relative rarity in the Gulf, but also because it was hosted in conjunction with Warehouse 421, an arts center in Abu Dhabi, as part of
an ongoing critical research project, "Stepping Away: Performance as
Practice in the Non-West." By aligning the Foundation with support
of local artists and of locally based research around contemporary
artistic practice, Jurkute and her colleagues at Alserkal, like Antonia
Carver at Art Jameel, are creating a new space for Gulf-based arts
criticism and practice.

Other projects at Alserkal that emphasize local and regional talent
while engaging with globally important questions include the development of a platform for opinion essays and responses to public programming written by local artists, writers and creative thinkers who
bring regional perspectives to diverse topics such as urban development, sustainability, cultural production and gender roles in Gulf society. In collaboration with Expo 2020, such conversation took place
through a wider platform with the launch of Cultural Conversations,
in which "UAE-based poets, artist collectives, and academics as well

as international urban theorists, artists, and diplomats ... debate pertinent topics through immersive experiences, artist interventions, informal conversations, and performances" (Zawya, 2021). The growth of this type of initiative offers the potential of another venue for critical conversation, rooted in contemporary artistic practice, in the Gulf region and also opens the doors for cross-disciplinary collaboration around topics of cultural significance in the region and beyond. As Jurkute explained in a 2020 interview, one of the goals of the programming offered by the Alserkal Arts Foundation is to respect and engage with the

> transnational nature of Dubai as a city, which is influenced by two symptoms of postmodern time: migration and mobility. Dubai is not so much about roots as it is about routes. Dubai and its surrounding cities are home to over 200 nationalities from multiple diasporas with various histories, values, and cultures. This is where arts and culture are so powerful: creating those bridges and providing a platform to bring us together.
>
> (Noor, 2020)

References

Al Hashemi, Z. (2018). Interview with the artist conducted by the author.

Al Hashemi, Z. (n.d.). 'Urban phantasmagoria: Cuadro gallery 2014–2016'. [Online] Available at: http://zeinabalhashemi.com/project-4-forte-1 [Accessed February 28, 2022].

Alsaden, A. (2021). 'Monira Al Qadiri dives deep into oil'. *Ocula Magazine.* March 3, 2021. [Online]. Available at: https://ocula.com/magazine/conversations/monira-al-qadiri-dives-deep-into-oil/ [Accessed January 27, 2022].

Art Jameel. (2022). 'History.' [Online] Available at: https://artjameel.org/about/history/ [Accessed January 31, 2022].

Ayad, M. (2016). 'Radhika Khimji'. *Artforum.* [Online] Available at: https://www.artforum.com/picks/radhika-khimji-59817 [Accessed January 26, 2022].

Binder, P. and Haupt, G. (2010). 'Radhika Khimji: Safe landings'. *Nafas.* [Online] Available at: https://universes.art/en/nafas/articles/2010/radhika-khimji [Accessed January 26, 2022].

DeTurk, S. (2020). 'Dubai's Alserkal Avenue: Cultural district or cultural diaspora?' In Wakefield, S. ed. *Museums of the Arabian Peninsula: Historical Developments and Contemporary Discourses.* London and New York: Routledge, pp. 160–172.

Elsheshtawy, Y., Ed. (2011). *The Evolving Arab City: Modernity and Urban Development*. London and New York: Routledge.

Khaleejesque. (2021). 'Walking paths: How is artist, writer and founder of culturist blog Hind Mezaina reconnecting with Dubai?' [Online] Available at: https://khaleejesque.me/2021/08/08/how-hind-mezaina-is-reconnecting-with-dubai/ [Accessed January 27, 2022].

Khimji, R. (n.d.). 'Artist's website'. [Online] Available at: https://www.radhikakhimji.com/ [Accessed January 26, 2022].

Molotch, H. and Ponzini, D., Eds. (2019). *The New Arab Urban: Gulf Cities of Wealth, Ambition and Distress*. New York: New York University Press.

Noor, T. (2020). 'Conversation with Vilma Jurkute, Alserkal'. [Online] Available at: https://iisforinstitute.icaphila.org/posts/conversation-with-vilma-jurkute-alserkal [Accessed January 31, 2022].

Seaman, A. (2018). 'Co-lab at Louvre Abu Dhabi'. [Online] Available at: https://annaseaman.net/blog/co-lab-at-louvre-abu-dhabi [Accessed February 28, 2022].

Stoby, A. (2009). 'Orientalism, globalization and commoditization: The artwork of Radhika Khimji'. *Muraqqa*. October 2009. [Online] Available at: http://muraqqa.org/radhika-r-khimji.html [Accessed January 13, 2022].

Tashkeel. (2021). 'Wonder land'. [Online] Available at: https://tashkeel.org/exhibitions/wonder-land [Accessed January 27, 2022].

Tripp, A. (2019). *Seeking Legitimacy: Why Arab Autocracies Adopt Women's Rights*. Cambridge: Cambridge University Press.

Vali, M. (2018). *Crude*. Dubai: Art Jameel.

Zawya. (2021). 'Alserkal and Expo 2020 join forces to create a new programme'. [Online] Available at: https://www.zawya.com/mena/en/press-releases/story/Alserkal_and_Expo_2020_join_forces_to_create_a_new_programme_Cultures_in_Conversation-ZAWYA20210908102456/ [Accessed January 31, 2022].

4   Cultural Diplomacy

Cultural Diplomacy

The use of the arts as a means of burnishing the international image of the Gulf countries as well as a driver of post-oil economies in Qatar, Saudi Arabia and the UAE is an established phenomenon. Natalia Grincheva (2013) describes this trend as the "use of diplomacy in promoting culture, resulting in a potentially greater awareness and interaction among various players, states, and individuals" (p. 39) and the term cultural diplomacy has become a standard descriptor of such activity. Lee Davidson and Leticia Pérez-Castellanos (2018) note the critical importance of traveling exhibitions for the advancement of cultural diplomacy and Alex Aubry (2020) explains that "For Gulf nations, like others before them, international Expos can be seen as an exercise in branding" (p. 221). Participation in high-profile biennials, such as the Venice Biennale, functions similarly and Gulf countries have been increasingly present in these events over the past two decades.

What has received less scholarly attention are the ways in which women are leading the cultural organizations central to this development. As Carol Malt (2007) notes in her pioneering study of the role of women as museum professionals in the Middle East,

> Museums can provide opportunities and empowerment for women in many ways: through employment, through reinterpretation of the patriarchal bias of collections and attributions, through increased exhibits of objects created by and related to women, through usage of the museum facility to teach their history, through literacy programmes and by providing economic benefit from the sale of women's museum-related publications and art.
>
> (p. 55)

DOI: 10.4324/9781003197119-5

Although Malt's study was focused specifically on museums, similar opportunities and benefits can be seen through women's participation in a variety of arts and cultural organizations, including galleries, heritage sites, art fairs and biennials. As Noha Mellor (2010) explains, there is a need to acknowledge women's participation in these sectors as evidence of their growing influence in the Arab world:

> We still measure female empowerment, by and large, by women's attainments in the economic, political, and educational spheres, such as employment, access to the labor market, and the number of female legislators, ministers, parliamentarians, or other decision-making offices. It is only recently that women's participation in the cultural field has begun to gain recognition as an important barometer to measure female empowerment. This field provides a vital platform for women to express their views about their identity and their rights within conservative societies not fully accepting of the role of women as culture producers.
>
> (p. 7)

It is thus critical to understand and assess their participation in this sphere throughout the region. This chapter uses four examples of women's high-profile participation in the contemporary art, museum and heritage sectors, focusing on Bahrain, Qatar, the UAE and the participation of Gulf countries in the Venice Biennale, to begin that process of understanding and assessment. In all cases, the reader will note that many of the women profiled have linkages to the royal families of the country; this is not uncommon in the monarchical societies of the Gulf where it is often the royal families that both lead the way in cultural initiatives and that encourage female members of the family to take leading roles in these high-profile ventures.

Bahrain

In his study of the ways that international exhibitions and cultural collaborations have contributed to Bahrain's cultural diplomacy efforts, Alex Aubry (2020) observes that "In Bahrain, a robust women-led arts and cultural infrastructure is contributing to conversations about meaningful inclusion within the museum field and cultural diplomacy" (p. 213). The woman most directly responsible for these efforts, through her own initiatives and through her leadership of a largely female team of arts and culture professionals, is Shaikha Mai bint Mohammed Al Khalifa, the President of the Bahrain Authority for

Culture and Antiquities (BACA). In this role, as well as in her previous position as founder of the Shaikh Ebrahim bin Mohammed Al Khalifa Center for Culture and Research, Shaikha Mai has led efforts both to preserve and celebrate Bahrain's cultural heritage and to link the Kingdom with the international community through the exchange of exhibitions, symposia and research programs. In a 2018 interview with Aubry, Shaikha Mai explained this strategy as a part of her vision for the development of BACA and its institutions (notably the Bahrain National Museum): "Now we are rethinking what the museum means today, particularly in terms of broadening our reach by forming networks with cultural organisations and institutions across the world" (Aubry, 2020, p. 145). These networks have led to partnerships with institutions in Russia, Italy, the United Kingdom and the United States among others. Shaikha Mai's personal participation in international conferences and symposia related to arts and cultural heritage has been central to these efforts; as Aubry explains,

> Part of BACA's strategy to create a network of cultural institutions and individuals has been through its participation in international forums. Over the last two decades Shaikha Mai has spoken as conferences, where she has met with policymakers and experts in the cultural field to identify key challenges and opportunities for collaboration.
>
> (pp. 145–146)

This personal involvement in the solicitation and nurturing of partnerships is a key component of the strategy that has helped BACA to position itself as an important asset to the Kingdom's diplomatic efforts.

What is particularly intriguing about Shaikha Mai's approach to the development of Bahrain's cultural landscape is the way in which various strands of past and present are woven together in the initiatives she and her team champion. During her tenure with BACA, both Pearling, Testimony of an Island Economy (Muharraq Pearling Path) and the Dilmun Burial Mounds have been inscribed as UNESCO World Heritage sites (in 2012 and 2019, respectively), highlighting the archaeological and heritage significance of the Kingdom's history. Also during her tenure, Bahrain saw its first national participation in the Venice Architecture Biennale in 2010 (for which it won the Golden Lion) and in the Venice Art Biennale in 2016, a sign of the Kingdom's investment in global contemporary art and architecture. These diverse efforts are reflective of the global connectedness fostered by Shaikha

Mai and carried forward by a member of the younger generation of Gulf arts and culture professionals, Shaikha Hala Bint Mohammed Al Khalifa. A Bahraini born in London and educated in the USA and UK, Shaikha Hala worked at the Qatar Museums Authority before returning to Bahrain to lead the Culture and Arts Directorate at BACA. A practicing fine artist herself, Shaikha Hala is especially concerned with developing local talent in the arts and design fields and sees the cross-cultural exchange as a means to that end. In an interview given in 2017, Shaikha Hala described her motivation for organizing a workshop in Paris for Bahraini art students:

> We can't expect young Bahrainis to envision a career in the arts or museums if we don't expose them to those fields. International workshops such as this one not only introduce Bahraini students to diverse artistic practices, but also to different cultures.
>
> (Aubry, 2020, p. 155)

By creating travel opportunities and hands-on workshops dedicated to creative and cultural exchange, Shaikha Hala pushes the cultural diplomacy practiced by Shaikha Mai in new directions. Not only will the transfer of objects serve to encourage cross-cultural dialogue, but the engagement of young Bahraini creatives with their counterparts globally will offer new opportunities for education and dialogue.

Qatar

Sheikha Al Mayassa bint Hamad bin Khalifa Al Thani, Chairperson of Qatar Museums, regularly appears on art world lists of top collectors; the reputed $1 billion acquisition budget that she controls assures her ongoing status as a figure of interest for the contemporary art market. The ruling Al Thani family (Sheikha Al Mayassa is the sister of the Emir) has been behind several high-profile purchases in recent years, notably the 2012 acquisition of Cezanne's *The Card Players* for a reported $250 million. Beyond the lavish spending, what is far more interesting about Sheikha Al Mayassa's role within the Al Thani family's drive to put Qatar on the map as an arts and culture destination is the way in which she has merged an interest in contemporary Western art, architecture and design with a commitment to developing local, Qatari talent. Her approach has been less to segregate the high-profile commissions of art world stars such as Richard Serra and Damien Hirst from the creation of heritage sites and local opportunities, but rather to find ways to link emerging Qatari artists and designers to projects that also incorporate international practitioners.

In a 2021 interview with the *Financial Times*, Sheikha Al Mayassa discussed her strategy for developing a local creative culture:

> I really believe it takes a quarter of a century for people to fully feel the impact of any sort of investment. We've done 15 years; for the next 10, we're focusing on the creative economy. We're trying to nurture that and [make] a community of creators. And you need the foundations; that can't be artificial or superficial. It has to be organically built.
>
> (Shollenbarger, 2021)

Some of this work is accomplished outside of the marquee institutions of Qatar Museums (Museum of Islamic Art, Mathaf), through projects such as the members-only Culture Pass (CP) Club in downtown Doha, a project that includes 14 interconnected townhouses designed by a mix of international names (Diane von Furstenberg, India Madhavi) and local talent (Wadha Al Hajri, Aisha Al-Sowaidi). While the project may seem a stretch of mandate for a museum authority, curator Whitney Robinson sees it as part of Qatar Museums' particular strategy of engagement beyond the typical remit for such an institution: "Qatar Museums doesn't act like a museum organisation; it's much more like a national endowment for the arts, or a national trust. By that definition, almost anything can come under its aegis" (Shollenbarger, 2021). Through an expansive approach to programming and development, Sheikha Al Mayassa opens possibilities for engaging Qataris with arts and culture outside of the traditional spaces of a museum, offering new opportunities for educating a new generation of artists, designers and creative professionals in the emirate.

Like Shaikha Mai bint Mohammed Al Khalifa in Bahrain, Sheikha Al Mayassa has also created a powerful team at Qatar Museums, many of whom are women, including several other members of the Al Thani family. Among this group, Sheikha Reem Al Thani stands out for her leadership in the utilization of technology as key engagement strategy in museum and exhibition design. After her graduation from Virginia Commonwealth University in Qatar, Sheikha Reem, who serves as Qatar Museums Director of Exhibitions, earned a master's degree in adaptive reuse interior architecture from the Rhode Island School of Design in 2015. As an undergraduate, she interned at Mathaf while the museum was still in its formative stages and through that experience became interested in the role of digital technologies in shaping museum and exhibition design (Noor, 2021). Sheikha Reem was part of a generation of Qataris who came of age during a time between the closing of the original National Museum in 1996 and the opening of the Museum of Islamic Art in 2006 when the country did not have any museum spaces, a gap that she sees reflected in a lack of awareness of possibilities for museum design:

> The National Museum closing in the nineties had a huge impact. I was part of that last group of students to go into the National Museum as a young visitor. I have those memories of my experience there. The students, from 1996 until the Islamic Museum opened, had no museum experience. It is now our mission to build audiences and professional capacity as well, in the museum sector. It is a great challenge because nobody was studying museum gallery design. But now that you can see a trajectory for your country, a lot of people started going abroad to study this. What is a social experience here? We think about that all the time. The museum is a social experience, a family experience, an educational experience.
>
> (Whitewall, 2020)

Sheikha Reem sees the opportunity for Qatar Museums to use the relative blank slate of the country's exhibition history to utilize technology to develop new strategies for exhibitions and visitor engagement, an opportunity hastened by the COVID-19 pandemic:

> As I see it, going digital offers two opportunities for cultural institutions: growing our audience beyond the confines of our physical museum space and enhancing our mission to preserve and share the stories of the content we curate and preserve for future generations.
>
> (Noor, 2021)

On working at the intersection of art, technology and exhibition design, Sheikha Reem is forging a path for Qatar Museums to push the boundaries of what it means to create effective and compelling visitor experiences in the twenty-first-century museum.

Several scholars have critiqued the prominent role played by members of the royal family in the development of Qatar Museums, as well as the organization'sreliance on expatriate museum. As Serena Iervolino (2020) explains, "Qatar's state museum sector lacks any distance from the government/ruling family, epitomizing ... the national cultural policy archetype of the 'engineer' state" (p. 71). This cultural policy strategy leads, in Iervolino's argument, to a situation in which the Qatari government (royal family) retains control over the country's museum development strategy, in opposition to the museum "franchise" model employed in, for example, Abu Dhabi and discussed extensively by Sarina Wakefield (2020), yet still has not led to the desired organic, growth from within that Sheikha Al Mayassa expresses a desire for. Yet, Iervolino sees the possibility of such growth occurring if Qataris are provided with training opportunities that privilege locally relevant museological strategies:

> A more organic and indigenous development of Qatar's museum sector may only be achieved when a 'critical mass' of *locally trained* Qataris will legitimately occupy leadership positions and introduce alternative museological forms ... To transform Qatar's museum ecosystem, I contend, it is vital to introduce a training provision aiming to develop a critical praxis that questions internationally accepted museum forms and standards, promotes appropriate and critical museologies, and favours an ethical and reflexive practice.
>
> (p. 80)

While Iervolino does not see the establishment of such indigenous training and praxis as a likely outcome for Qatar and other Gulf states, I believe that the path of development in the museum sector is not yet fully defined and that the role played by a younger generation of khaleeji museum leaders, particularly women, may lead to more locally inflected and community-engaged outcomes within the sector.

UAE

The emirate of Sharjah in the UAE does not get as much media attention as its flashy neighbor, Dubai. Nor does it boast the spectacular range of international museums that are taking shape on Saadiyat Island in Abu Dhabi. However, under the leadership of the Ruler of Sharjah, His Highness Sheikh Dr. Sultan bin Mohammed Al Qasimi, the emirate has developed an extensive network of cultural institutions, including 16 museums and the Sharjah Art Foundation (SAF), sponsor of the Sharjah Biennial. Both the Sharjah Museums Authority and the SAF are run by Emirati women: Manal Ataya and Sheikha Hoor Al Qasimi, respectively.

Sharjah Museums Authority was established in 2006 by Sheikh Sultan and oversees the operation of 16 museums in the emirate, ranging from an aquarium to an archaeological museum, to the Museum of Islamic Civilization and to the Sharjah Art Museum. Manal Ataya earned a master's degree in Museum Studies at Harvard University and initially served as Deputy Director of Sharjah Museums Authority before her appointment to the directorship in 2008. Since taking over the leadership of the authority, Ataya has overseen the opening of new museums and focused on increasing the audience for the institutions in her portfolio. She has been instrumental in raising the profile of Sharjah Museums within the community and throughout the UAE, notably through the use of social media and community partnerships to increase awareness of the resources offered by the museums. While COVID-19 lockdowns forced the Sharjah Museums, as with other institutions, to rely on virtual tours, online workshops and other technology-enabled means of connecting with their audience, Ataya sees the physical experience of the museum visit as critical:

> I believe visiting museums is such a unique, highly personal experience to each individual, and can keep unfolding over time. For a lot of people, a museum is not a space to look at art – it's a place for community events and social get togethers, so that's the part technology is not able to really help us bring back.
>
> (Brunt, 2020)

Community engagement is an area in which Ataya has particularly invested during her time at Sharjah Museums. This work has included the development of strong educational programs in each institution, particularly at the flagship Sharjah Art Museum and Sharjah Museum of Islamic Civilization. Because the museums of Sharjah are more likely to be visited by local audiences than international tourists, Ataya has emphasized connections with schools and universities, providing arts and cultural programming and workshops that supplement the curriculum and introduce students to the museums, an introduction that hopefully will lead to family engagement as well. Recognizing the need for museum educators to lead such initiatives, Ataya sought, in her words, "to hire more people, more specialists, trained education specialists to deliver programs, to start creating and designing programs for children and for families" (Swan, 2021). In recent years, she has emphasized the establishment of programs and facilities to support accessibility within the Sharjah Museums, from physical alterations to accommodate wheelchair users to the initiation of programs such as providing tours in sign language for hearing impaired visitors and the establishment of the "Autism Friendly Museums" program

(Krishna Kumar, 2021). Through a series of opinion essays written for *The National*, one of the UAE's leading English-language newspapers, Ataya has promoted the work being done at Sharjah Museums in terms of accessibility and community engagement, helping to focus attention on the role that museums can play in education for the UAE's citizens and residents, not just as tourist attractions.

Also in Sharjah, Sheikha Hoor Al Qasimi has, since 2003, led the development of the Emirate as a key venue for contemporary art in the Gulf. The daughter of the ruler of Sharjah, Sheikha Hoor earned her BFA from the Slade School of Fine Art in London and her MA in curating contemporary art from the Royal College of Art in London. Her work as a curator began during her time at the Slade, in the early 2000s, and she co-curated Sharjah Biennial 6 in 2003, continuing as director of the biennial since that time. In 2009, she established the SAF which includes under its umbrella of activities not only the biennial, but a wide-ranging exhibition program, film programming, artist residencies, educational workshops and symposia, notably the March Meeting. The Foundation's headquarters and exhibition spaces in the cultural and historic center of Sharjah are an important example of adaptive reuse of existing structures mixed with purpose-built exhibition and meeting spaces, an urban design strategy that has been unfortunately lacking in other emirates in the UAE and in other Gulf countries. Sheikha Hoor has contributed to other innovative architectural reclamation projects, reclaiming an old ice storage and factory building in Kalba as a site for the biennial and other SAF activities and overseeing the restoration of the 1978 Flying Saucer building in Sharjah as an arts center. As Chair of the Board of the recently established Sharjah Architecture Triennial, she is poised to continue to develop Sharjah as the center for conversations around architecture in the region and beyond.

It is Sheikha Hoor's curatorial vision, however, that has established her as a critical figure in the contemporary art world. The Sharjah Biennial and SAF are unique in the Gulf for their inclusion of a broad range of artists, many from the Global South, whose works often both challenge and reflect the culture of the region. In 2003, when Sheikha Hoor first curated the biennial, she initiated the practice of commissioning artists to create work specifically for the biennial; in 2005, this practice extended to the introduction of longer-term artist residencies (Mack, 2012). Bringing international artists to Sharjah for extended periods of time and encouraging them to create work that specifically engaged with the history and geography of the emirate, Sheikha Hoor and the SAF have contributed to the development of bodies of work that reflect the complex nature of UAE society, with its vast population of expatriates, and the history of the emirate as a crossroads of multiple cultures. Sometimes these works receive near-universal acclaim, as was the case with Wael Shawky's piece *Dictums 10:120* (2011–2013), performed at Sharjah Biennial 11. The piece grew out of Shawky's residency at SAF and involved a collaborative process in which the artist and various members of the biennial staff, most of whom were Pakistani,

> took apart the Biennial's rhetoric in order to construct a song. In a move that highlights the historic exchange of labour and culture between the Gulf region and South Asia, Shawky travelled to Karachi, in Pakistan, to record the song with renowned qawwals Fareed Ayaz and Abu Muhammad. During the opening week of Sharjah Biennial 11, the two qawwals, along with 30 additional men, perform the song in an alleyway outside the exhibition halls; a trace of their presence remains as an audio track that plays in the space throughout the duration of the Biennial.
>
> (Sharjah Art Foundation, 2013)

Other interventions were not well-received, particularly by local audiences in Sharjah, notably Mustapha Benfoldil's contribution to Sharjah Biennial 10, *Maportaliche/Ecritures sauvages* (*It Has No Importance/Wild Writings*, 2011), which was removed soon after its installation due to complaints about its blasphemous nature. The incident, which was linked by many in the international art community to the subsequent departure of the biennial's artistic director, Jack Persekian, exemplified the fine line that Sheikha Hoor has to walk in leading a contemporary arts organization in what is, arguably, the most conservative emirate in the UAE. In a 2012 interview, Sheikha Hoor discussed the difficulties inherent in exhibiting contemporary art, particularly art with a political message, in Sharjah, where multiple audiences have diverse perspectives and boundaries: "I don't want to lose our audience. If we did, what would be our role here? We wouldn't be the Sharjah Art Foundation. We might as well be anywhere in the world" (Mack, 2012).

Following the controversy over the removal of Benfodil's work and Persekian's departure, Sheikha Hoor continued to guide the biennial and the SAF toward critical engagement with issues of politics, race, gender and representation in contemporary art while attending to the interests of local audiences as well. This has led to the programming as diverse as a retrospective of the work of Emirati artist Hassan Sharif (1951–2016), considered the first Emirati conceptual artist and one of the founders of the contemporary art movement in the UAE, and an exhibition of the work of Egyptian feminist artist Amal Kenawy (1974–2012). The annual March Meetings, initially conceived as a corollary to the biennial exhibitions, now function as important symposia on issues in contemporary art, with a particular emphasis on the Global South. The ongoing development of this type of programming will ensure Sharjah's continued significance as a site for critical artistic investigation and discourse. Sheikha Hoor's commitment to this work was honored by the Asia Society of New York in 2020, when she was named as a "game changer" for her work

> to promote greater cultural understanding and exchange between artists, curators, cultural producers, and the public. She has given artists a platform that ranges across the Middle East, Africa, South Asia, and beyond, while working to bring international artworks and artists to residents of the UAE.

> (Asia Society, 2022)

Venice Biennale

Since its founding in 1895, the Venice Biennale has established itself as the premiere exhibition venue for contemporary art (as well as architecture, cinema, music, theater and dance), giving rise to dozens of biennials and triennials around the world. It is no surprise, then, that Gulf countries have sought to burnish their reputation as artistic hubs through participation in this critically important venue. By 2022, every GCC country except Qatar will have participated with a pavilion in the international art exhibition, though several countries have been more active in the architecture exhibition (established in 1980 and now held in alternate years when the art exhibition is not running). The UAE became the first Gulf country to host a national pavilion at the Venice Biennale in 2009 and has been the most consistent participant, in both the art and architecture exhibitions, since then. Saudi Arabia participated in the art exhibition in 2011 and 2019, Bahrain and Kuwait in 2013 and Oman's national pavilion debuted in 2022. In all cases, women have played key roles as artists and/or curators of

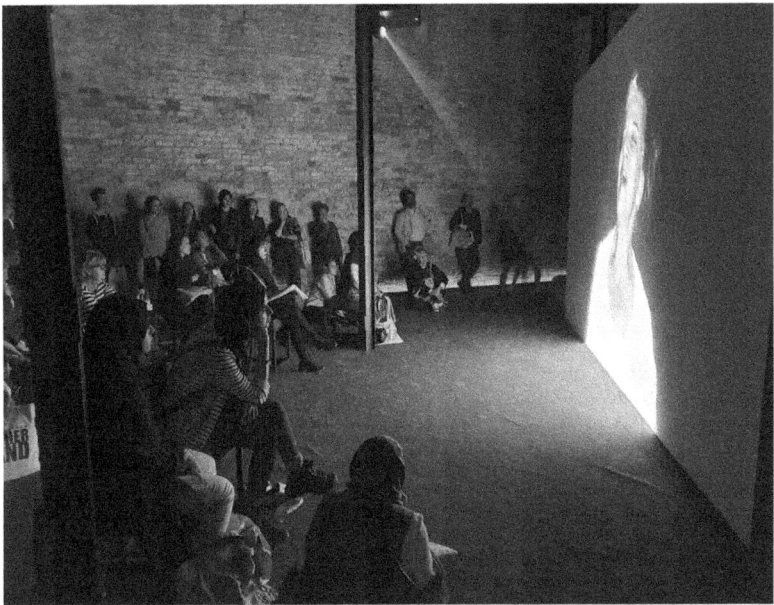

Figure 4.1 View of Nujoom Alghanem's video installation *Passage* in the United Arab Emirates pavilion at the 2019 Venice Biennale. Photograph by the author.

these exhibitions: Bahrain's 2013 pavilion featured the artists Mariam Haji and Waheeda Mallulah; Kuwait's pavilion in the same year was curated by Ala Younis; Saudi Arabia's 2011 pavilion showcased the work of sisters Shadia and Raja Alem, while the country's second participation in 2019 presented sculpture by Zahrah Alghamdi; the UAE established its ongoing presence in Venice by showing photographs by Lamya Gargash in 2009. Women have also been key protagonists in these countries' pavilions for the architecture exhibition, though an examination of their roles in that arena is beyond the scope of this study.

The choice of women artists (or, in the case of Kuwait, a woman curator) to anchor the inaugural presentations of these Gulf countries in a prestigious international contemporary arts exhibit speaks to the role that the Biennale plays in the construction of soft-power and cultural diplomacy for many of the participating countries (Berlanda, 2020; Mohammad, 2019). Elizabeth Derderian's (2022) description of the rationale for the UAE's selection of Lamya Gargash (born 1982) for the 2009 exhibition highlights the role that her citizenship and choice of medium played in making her a good fit for the country's aspirational desires for the pavilion:

> Selecting Gargash offered a number of advantages: She is an Emirati citizen, thus representing the nation's young and emerging talent. Gargash works in photography, a popular medium and one strongly associated with contemporary art ... In the context of the pavilion, Gargash represented the UAE's bright cultural future.
>
> (p. 27)

As important as her Emirati citizenship and engaging medium might be, the fact that Gargash was also a woman artist helped to signify to the international audience of the Biennale that the UAE rejected the patriarchal stereotypes associated with the Middle East and represented a new egalitarianism, at least in terms of outward presentation of opportunity for women artists. Much the same strategy could be attributed to Saudi Arabia in its choice to showcase the women artists Shadia and Raja Alem (born 1960 and 1970, respectively) in their inaugural pavilion in 2011. By continuing to foreground the presence of women artists and curators in their follow-up presentations, Saudi Arabia and the UAE (the only two Gulf countries that, at the time of this writing, had participated more than once in the Biennale's art exhibition) provide examples of the ways in which gender can be used as a signaling device for countries to present themselves as open and cosmopolitan settings for cultural diversity. An examination of the 2019 iteration of the Saudi Arabia pavilion at the Venice Biennale will explain this further.

The 2019 Saudi Arabia Pavilion at the Venice Biennale featured a site-specific work titled *After Illusion* (2019) by the Jeddah-based sculptor and land artist Zahrah Al Ghamdi (born 1977) and was curated by Eiman Elgibreen (born 1981), an artist and art historian on the faculty of Princess Nourah University in Riyadh. Al Ghamdi's installation was crafted from over 50,000 pieces of leather which were cut, burned and shaped into organic forms reminiscent of the landscape in which the artist grew up. Some of these forms were attached to hanging textiles, others piled on the floor of the pavilion. The white draperies were backlit, contributing to a sense that the forms were moving across them in a life-like manner. The forms could also be squeezed, producing individual sounds that were played over an audio system and further engaging the audience with the tactile nature of the work. The piece

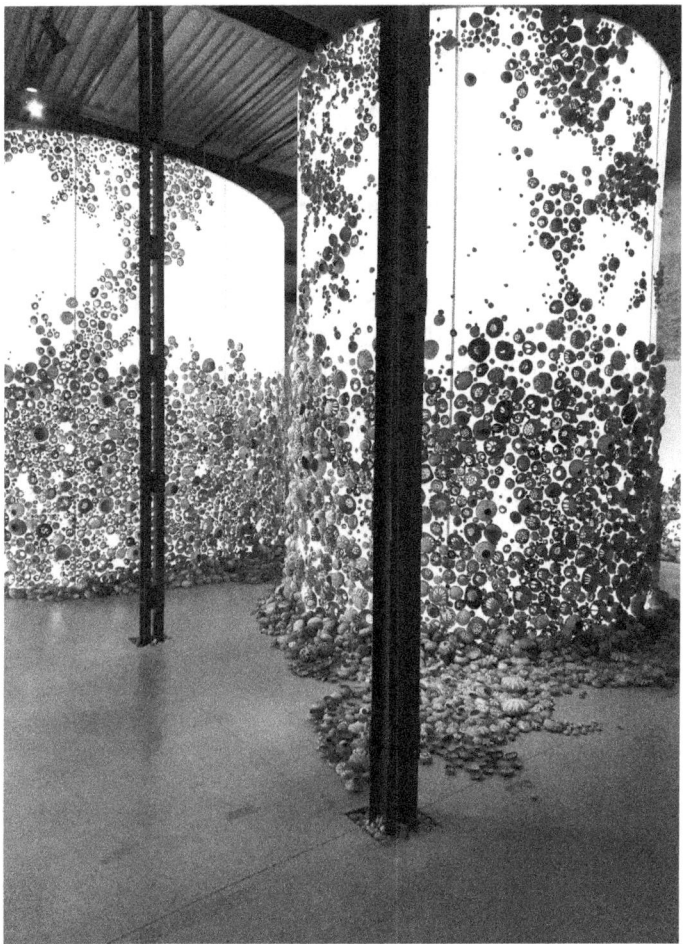

Figure 4.2 Installation view of the Saudi Arabia pavilion at the 2019 Venice Biennale showing a detail of Zahrah Al Ghamdi's *After Illusion*. Photograph by the author.

speaks to issues of memory, nostalgia, craft traditions and connection to the landscape, all themes Al Ghamdi has explored frequently in her work. By addressing such universal themes, albeit with a personal geographic and cultural resonance for this Saudi artist, Al Ghamdi provided the visitor to the Saudi pavilion with an experience both global and specific. Curator Elgibreen emphasized this accessibility in her explanation for Al Ghamdi's selection:

> She was chosen because her handmade pieces, and the many emotions she undergoes, speak to the pavilion's proposed theme. [Her work] carries the ability to use the past in building a future. While witnessing recent changes in the Kingdom, Saudi artists are envisioning the optimistic future of the Saudi art scene.
>
> (Mohammad, 2019)

While many reviewers praised the aesthetics of Al Ghamdi's installation, few ignored the larger context for Saudi's return to the Venice stage, coming less than a year after the government-sanctioned murder of dissident Saudi journalist Jamal Khashgoggi (Harris, 2019; Mohammad, 2019). The choice of a female artist to represent the Kingdom at this juncture allowed the pavilion's curator and commissioner to shift the conversation from some of the more troubling aspects of Saudi's past and present and instead to focus on the future; in Elgibreen's words,

> the pavilion helped visitors see for themselves how matured the contemporary art scene is. Saudi artists are creating positive change, while balancing their national heritage and global developments. They are reconsidering the recent shift in the status quo of the Kingdom. These rapid-paced changes are motivating artists to re-imagine the future of Saudi art.
>
> (Mohammad, 2019)

References

Asia Society. (2022). 'Hoor Al Qasimi: For transforming the arts across the Middle East and beyond'. [Online] Available at: https://asiasociety.org/asia-game-changer-awards/hoor-al-qasimi [Accessed February 10, 2022].

Aubry, A. (2020). 'Beyond museum walls: Envisioning a role for Gulf institutions as instigators of cross-cultural diplomacy'. In Wakefield, S. ed. *Museums of the Arabian Peninsula: Historical Developments and Contemporary Discourses.* Abingdon and New York: Routledge, pp. 140–159.

Berlanda, T. (2020). 'World stage: World Expos and Venice Biennales are significant platforms for international dialogue, but are also an arena of soft power and political posturing'. *Architectural Review* (1471), pp. 16–20. Available at: https://search-ebscohost-com.ezproxy.sju.edu/login.aspx?direct=true&db=aph&AN=143107616&site=ehost-live [Accessed February 11, 2022].

Brunt, L. (2020). 'Meet the woman shaping Sharjah's museums'. *Sekka*. April 29, 2020. [Online] Available at: https://sekkamag.com/2020/04/29/meet-the-woman-shaping-sharjahs-museums/ [Accessed February 7, 2022].

Davidson, L. and Pérez-Castellanos, L. (2018). *Cosmopolitan Ambassadors: International Exhibitions, Cultural Diplomacy and the Polycentral Museum*. Wilmington, Delaware: Vernon Press.

Derderian, E. (2022). 'Exhibiting tolerance: Citizenship, contingency and contemporary art in the UAE Pavilion, 2009–2017'. In Bouzas, A. M. and Casini, L. eds. *Migration in the Making of the Gulf Space: Social, Political, and Cultural Dimensions*. Oxford and New York: Berghahn Books, pp. 21–42.

Grincheva, N. (2013). 'Cultural diplomacy 2.0: Challenges and opportunities in museum international practices'. *Museum & Society*, 11(1), pp. 39–49.

Harris, G. (2019). 'Saudi Arabia returns to Venice Biennale after eight-year hiatus'. *The Art Newspaper*. April 9, 2019. [Online] Available at: https://www.theartnewspaper.com/2019/04/09/saudi-arabia-returns-to-venice-biennale-after-eight-year-hiatus [Accessed February 11, 2022].

Iervolino, S. (2020). 'Qatar's accelerated museum developmental model: Rhetoric, actors and expertise'. In Wakefield, S. ed. *Museums of the Arabian Peninsula: Historical Developments and Contemporary Discourses*. Abingdon and New York: Routledge, pp. 67–84.

Krishna Kumar, N. P. (2020). 'Two Sharjah museums awarded the global "accessible for disability certificate"'. *Al Arabiya*. November 13, 2020. [Online] Available at: https://english.alarabiya.net/life-style/art-and-culture/2020/11/13/Two-Sharjah-museums-awarded-the-Accessible-for-Disability-Certificate- [Accessed February 7, 2022].

Mack, J. (2012). 'Sheikha Hoor Al-Qasimi'. *Art in America*, 100(6), p. 93. [Online] Available at: https://search-ebscohost com.ezproxy.sju.edu/login.aspx?direct=true&db=edsgao&AN=edsgcl.295076504&site=eds-live [Accessed February 10, 2022].

Mellor, N. (2010). 'Empowering women through the arts'. *Middle East Institute Viewpoints: Creative Arab Women*. July 1, 2010. [Online] Available at: https://www.mei.edu/publications/introduction-state-arts-middle-east-volume-vi-creative-arab-women [Accessed January 13, 2022].

Mohammad, A. (2019). 'At the Venice Biennale, a world stage for soft power, rivals Iran and Saudi Arabia vie to put their best feet forward'. *Artnet*. May 20, 2019. [Online] Available at: https://news.artnet.com/art-world/venice-biennale-iran-saudia-arabia-1549042 [Accessed February 11, 2022].

Noor, N. (2021). 'Qatar's Sheikha Reem Al-Thani on bringing Arab art and museums into the future'. *Vogue Arabia*. February 3, 2021. [Online] Available at: https://en.vogue.me/culture/sheikha-reem-al-thani-vogue-arabia-interview/ [Accessed February 2, 2022].

Sharjah Art Foundation. (2013). 'Dictums 10:120'. [Online] Available at: http://sharjahart.org/sharjah-art-foundation/projects/dictums-10120   [Accessed February 10, 2022].

Shollenbarger, M. (2021). 'Sheikha Al Mayassa Al Thani, the woman behind Doha's bid to become a cultural hub'. *Financial Times.* November 30, 2021. [Online] Available at: https://www.ft.com/content/60587fb2-d1de-4f2f-8aa3-b0991f98bf49 [Accessed February 2, 2022].

Swan, M. (2021). 'Manal Ataya: Director of Sharjah's museums embraces an educational role'. *Al-Fanar Media.* May 28, 2021. [Online] Available at: https://www.al-fanarmedia.org/2021/05/manal-ataya-director-of-sharjahs-museums-embraces-an-educational-role/ [Accessed February 7, 2022].

Wakefield, S. (2020). *Cultural Heritage, Transnational Narratives and Museum Franchising in Abu Dhabi.* Abingdon and New York: Routledge.

Whitewall. (2020). 'Sheikha Reem Al-Thani is thinking of the 21st century audience'. [Online] Available at: https://whitewall.art/art/sheikha-reem-al-thani-thinking-21st-century-audience [Accessed February 2, 2022].

5   Professional Development

Overview

The opportunities for professional training and development in the fine arts vary widely between Gulf countries, with some offering multiple avenues for professional development ranging from formal university degree programs to privately funded workshops, residencies and ateliers. This chapter focuses on the two countries with the greatest range of opportunities for university-based training and ongoing professional development in the fine arts: Saudi Arabia and the United Arab Emirates. However, a brief overview of the situation in other Gulf countries is warranted, as the education opportunities available in each have a substantive impact on the ability for women to emerge and mature as contemporary artists and arts professionals. As noted in the introduction to this volume, restrictions on travel, including travel for higher education, can put Gulf women at a substantial disadvantage in relation to their international peers when it comes to obtaining advanced training in the fine arts, art history or museum studies. Therefore, it is important to understand the local educational and professional development offerings available in each country to better understand the presence (or absence) of contemporary women artists in each locale.

Bahrain

As discussed in the first chapter of this volume, Bahrain has a wealth of cultural heritage sites and a strong national museum, setting the stage for its support of the fine arts as well. However, that support, in terms of education and exhibition opportunities for fine artists, has been somewhat limited. The University of Bahrain offers a bachelor's degree in fine arts and graphic design, but this combined program

DOI: 10.4324/9781003197119-6

does not offer the level of specialization that would benefit a student wishing to pursue a career as a professional artist. The Bahrain Arts Society was founded in 1983 to support local fine artists; however, it is no longer as active as some similar Gulf institutions (for example, the Emirates Fine Arts Society). Manama, the capital city of Bahrain, is home to several art galleries which do provide opportunities for local artists to exhibit their work, however, the preferred styles are often more traditional than cutting edge. Unfortunately, at the time of this writing, one of the most interesting new ventures in the contemporary arts scene, the art fair Art Bahrain Across Borders, which held its inaugural edition in 2016, is no longer operational; whether this represents a temporary hiatus due to COVID-19 or a permanent closure remains to be seen.

A relatively new, private university, the Royal University for Women, opened in Bahrain in 2006 and offers both undergraduate degrees in design and a Master of Fine Arts degree in Drawing and Painting through its College of Art and Design (RUW, n.d.). While the program curricula and faculty qualifications seem weighted more toward design than fine arts, it is possible that this institution will provide educational opportunities that support Bahraini women seeking to establish themselves as artists. Bahrain's participation in the Venice Biennale, while currently invested more in architecture than in art, also affords a platform for the training of future artists and curators in the Kingdom.

Kuwait

While Kuwait had one of the earliest modern art movements in the Gulf, government support for the arts has declined dramatically over the years and the country now offers few educational opportunities or professional associations for its artists. The American University of Kuwait offers an undergraduate program in graphic design and Kuwait University houses an undergraduate program in Visual Communication Design, but there are no fine arts degree programs in the country. Historically, the Sultan Gallery, often cited as the first Arab art gallery in the Gulf, functioned as an important center for Kuwaiti artists, serving as "a convergence point for not only artists and intellectuals exploring polemic issues on Arab society, but also the general public" until its closure in 1990 (Sultan Gallery, n.d.). The gallery was reopened in 2006 and continues to mount exhibitions that "advance a critical art discourse emerging in the country" (Sultan Gallery, n.d.). Women artists have been well-represented throughout the gallery's tenure, in shows ranging from a 1970 exhibition of work by the Iraqi sculptor Nuha Radi to a show of Kuwaiti artist Ghada AlKandari's figurative paintings in 2020.

The second important site for the exhibition of contemporary art in Kuwait is the Contemporary Art Platform (CAP), which was founded in 2011 and has consistently presented a strong program of shows by Kuwaiti and international artists. The gallery houses a library of art books and also supports an educational program of workshops, seminars and film screenings and states its mission to "play a role in establishing Kuwait as a contributor to the art world and fosters the next generation of art lovers in the region" (CAP, 2020). The gallery has hosted several important exhibitions of work by women artists, including Kuwaitis Shurooq Amin (see Chapter 2 of this volume for a discussion of the censorship of her work by Kuwaiti authorities), Zahra Al-Mahdi, Najeebah Al-Ghadban and Aseel AlYaqoub, among others. In 2015, CAP hosted the exhibition "Abolish 153", in support of the campaign to abolish article 153, which sanctions the murder of female relatives caught in adulterous acts, from Kuwait's penal code (Art Kuwait, 2015). The version of the exhibition at CAP (it has since been stage annually at other galleries) also marked the tenth anniversary of women's suffrage in Kuwait. Through exhibitions such as this and others, CAP has demonstrated a willingness to use contemporary art as a means to engage directly with social issues of importance to women in Kuwait and throughout the Gulf region.

Oman

Of all the GCC countries, Oman has, arguably, the least developed professional arts community and this absence of local educational and exhibition opportunities may explain the relative absence of Omani artists, male or female, in the contemporary art world. Historically, Oman was an important location on the Indian Ocean trade routes, resulting in a cross-cultural exchange between Europe (the Portuguese occupied Muscat from 1508 to 1648), the Indian subcontinent, East Africa and the Gulf. However, as Robert Kluijver (2013) recognizes "Oman's artistic community is strongly rooted within the country's cultural history, setting it apart from its counterparts in the Emirates, Qatar and Kuwait, which seem oriented abroad" (p. 129). This internal orientation may also be explained by the relatively low percentage of expatriates in Oman, in comparison to countries such as Qatar and the UAE. The cosmopolitan, global perspective valued in Doha and Dubai is not apparent in Muscat. Fine arts organizations in Oman began to emerge in the 1980s, with the opening of the Youth Art Studio, founded in 1980 as part of the Directorate General of Cultural and Youth Sports, the establishment of which "is regarded as the starting point for the Omani fine art movement" (Al-Yahyai, 2012; p. 3). The country's first university program in the arts, an arts education degree at Sultan Qaboos University was established in 1991 and the Omani Society of Fine Arts (OSFA) was created by the government in 1993. In her study of the history of women artists in Oman, Fakhriya Al-Yahyai (2012) highlights both the creation of the OSFA and the subsequent (1997) launch of annual exhibitions dedicated exclusively to Omani resident women artists as critical to the increasing number of women participating in the fine arts movement in Oman. Yet even this support has not resulted in substantial numbers of internationally recognized Omani women artists and within Oman itself the opportunities for both education in the fine arts and exhibition of contemporary art are limited. The arts education degree program at Sultan Qaboos University remains the only state-sponsored option for higher education in the visual arts (the university does offer separate programs in music and theater arts) and Muscat is home to only a few contemporary art galleries (notably Stal Gallery, Bait Muznah and Sarah Gallery). In 2004, the private Scientific College of Design was opened in Muscat, offering BA degrees in various fields including fine art and photography. Although the SCD received its accreditation from the Oman Academic Accreditation Authority in 2019, it appears to function more as a trade school than a university (similar to the private chain of Art Institutes in the United States). The 2022 inaugural participation of Oman in the Venice Biennale art exhibition may be a signal that the country is seeking to increase its focus on the contemporary visual arts. Omani art historian Aisha Stoby, who is curating the pavilion in Venice, is emerging as an important researcher and curator who is producing some of the first scholarships on the modern and contemporary art of Oman and other Gulf countries (NYUAD, 2022). If her work is able to introduce other scholars and curators to the work of artists in Oman, the opportunities for further research and exhibitions are rich.

Qatar

Like the UAE, Qatar moved in the 1990s to establish connections with several international universities which eventually set up branch campuses in Doha's Education City. In terms of arts education, the most significant of these campuses were those of University College London (which closed its Qatar branch in 2020) and Virginia Commonwealth University School of the Arts, which maintains a vibrant undergraduate program and developing graduate program as of this writing. At the undergraduate level, the Bachelor of Fine Arts (BFA) in Painting and Printmaking offers both Qatari and expatriate students the opportunity to develop a sound foundation in contemporary arts practice and prepare for a further student abroad (the MFA program at VCU is in design, rather than a fine arts discipline).

In 2014, Qatar Museums opened the Fire Station, an adaptive reuse project which saw a former civil defense facility repurposed as a space for artists' studios, a gallery, café and shop. The Fire Station supports an artist residency program that draws both international and local artists, including, importantly, graduates from the VCU programs. In this way, Qatar is providing an opportunity for ongoing professional development for alumni of the arts program who may not be able to continue their study abroad; several women graduates of the VCA programs have held residencies at the Fire Station (Fire Station, n.d.). The provision of studio space, as well as introduction to an international community of artists (both current and past artists in residence), is critical to the development of a professional network and sustainable practice for emerging artists. While previous initiatives, such as the independent Katara Art Center (founded in 2012), have attempted to generate this kind of grassroots, community-oriented arts environment in Qatar they have not been overwhelmingly successful. Katara Art Center came close to closing due to lack of funding in 2014; its current status, as of the time of the writing, is unclear (Milliard, 2014).

Saudi Arabia

As Saudi artist Ahmed Mater explains in an essay charting the development of the Saudi art scene in the latter half of the twentieth century, the presence of an open, government-supported arts sector in the Kingdom has been sporadic, tied to the geo-political situation of the country itself. As Mater (n.d.) writes,

> In many ways, this is a story told in reverse. Where one might hope, even expect, to see a progressive enlightenment – an art scene that gathers strength moving from early pioneers to popular awareness, with a growing infrastructure to support education and production – it has instead been a non-linear journey, punctured and stalled, gathering pace in closed communities though often limited and isolated in society at large.

This is not a narrative that yields an easy summation; like Saudi Arabia itself, it is large, complex and bears the imprint of many traditions and histories. However, certain elements within this story are of particular significance in terms of the role that women artists have played within the emerging Saudi contemporary art scene, and I will discuss two of these here: the Edge of Arabia initiative and the nascent Saudi biennial movement, specifically Desert X AlUla and Diriyah Biennale. It must be acknowledged that any discussion of the arts in Saudi Arabia is shadowed by the country's ongoing suppression of human rights, particularly the rights of women, and evidenced in a most egregious fashion by the 2018 murder of dissident journalist Jamal Khashoggi. While my discussion of women and contemporary art in Saudi Arabia does not specifically grapple with the tensions raised by the valorization of women artists in a country that still does not guarantee full agency to its female citizens, this is an important issue worthy of ongoing research and dialogue.

Edge of Arabia

The non-profit arts organization Edge of Arabia was founded by British artist Stephen Stapleton and Saudi artist Ahmed Mater, following their meeting at the Al-Meftaha Arts Village in Abha, KSA, in 2003. The group has been supported since its inception by major institutions in the region and beyond, including Art Jameel, the British Council, the Brooklyn Museum and many others and this support has enabled the production of forty exhibitions of work by Saudi and other Middle Eastern artists between 2008 and 2018, held in locations as varied as London, Venice, Jeddah and New York (Edge of Arabia, n.d.). Of particular interest in the context of this book is the first Edge of Arabia exhibition held in London at the Brunei Gallery of the School of Oriental and African Studies in 2008.

Beginning with the curatorial team of Stephen Stapleton, Ahmed Mater and Lulwah Al-Homoud, the exhibition quietly but forcefully asserted an essential role for Saudi women artists alongside their male counterparts. Of the 17 artists included in the exhibition, seven were women: Shadia and Raja Alem, Manal Al-Dowayan, Reem Al-Faisal, Lulwah Al-Homoud, Maha Malluh and Noha Al-Sharif. As discussed elsewhere in this volume, Shadia and Raja Alem would go on to represent Saudi Arabia at the Kingdom's first participation in the Venice Biennale in 2011; the works of Maha Malluh and Manal Al-Dowayan have been highlighted in Chapters 1 and 2 of this text, respectively.

The other three women artists included in the first Edge of Arabia exhibition have not gone on to have as extensive an exhibition history, however, works by both Reem Al-Faisal and Lulway Al-Homoud are included in the permanent collection of the Barjeel Art Foundation, one of the most significant private collections of modern and contemporary art from the Arab world. What is important about the Edge of Arabia exhibition, which subsequently traveled to Venice, Riyadh and Berlin after its run in London, is that the activity of women artists in Saudi Arabia was presented as a given; their works were not highlighted as anomalies, or overly concerned with issues of gender and identity but rather discussed on their own merits, as part of a "new creative movement within Saudi Arabia, responding to a range of themes: their personal relationship to the Islamic faith; the artist's voice in the media age; and the history, culture and ecology of the region" (Edge of Arabia, 2008). This participation sets the stage for an ongoing integration of women artists and curators into the newly emerging Saudi contemporary arts scene.

Saudi Biennials

While Saudi Arabia's participation in the international biennial circuit, headlined by the Venice Biennale, has been sporadic, the Kingdom has made an effort to develop its own biennial offerings as part of the drive to increase cultural tourism within the country and from outside its borders. Although the two efforts in this regard – Desert X AlUla and the Diriya Biennale – are new entrants to the field of global biennials, their foregrounding of women artists makes them worth considering in the context of this study.

Desert X AlUla held its inaugural exhibition in January 2020, just before the world essentially closed its borders due to the global pandemic and at a moment when Saudi Arabia's reputation on the world stage was at a low. Reviewing the show for the *New York Times*, Vivian Yee (2020) captured the tension inherent in the choice of the US-based Desert X art group to accept the Saudi government's offer to fund an offshoot of their land-art biennial exhibition in the Kingdom:

> Controversy ensued, as it tends to when Saudi Arabia — whose government has hacked the iPhone of one of the world's richest men, tortured dissidents, dismembered a critical journalist and helped ignite a humanitarian disaster in Yemen — overlaps with Western institutions.

Yet as Yee's review went on to make clear, such controversy was often eschewed by the artists, many of them women, who agreed to participate in the event. Saudi artist Manal Al-Dowayan was quoted as saying "They talked about building bridges. I don't know about that. We're just here making art" (Yee, 2020), while Sherin Guirguis, an Egyptian-American artist, focused on the opportunities for cultural exchange offered by the exhibition. Discussing a workshop and lecture series she participated in with local Saudi women weavers, Guirguis reflected on the potential for human connection to make an impact:

> From a Western perspective, it's very easy to look at the politics of a place and the government of a place, and to make those decisions to reject them, and the people who get affected are the people we claim to want to help. Will the work that I've done there make the world's smallest dent and help move things forward? I hope so.
>
> (Yee, 2020)

The appointment of two Saudi women, Raneem Farsi and Aya Alireza, as curators of Desert X AlUla and the prominent participation of women artists (Saudi and of other nationalities), ensured that the event would be seen as part of the Kingdom's drive toward opening its society, both internally and externally. By the second iteration of Desert X AlUla, held in winter 2022 and co-curated by Farsi and Reem Fadda, this message was clear. Reviewing the biennial for *Artnet News*, Rebecca Anne Proctor (2022) described the event as a "major part" of the ambitious Vision 2030 initiative sponsored by Crown Prince Mohamed bin Salman and focused her review more on the artworks than on the controversy surrounding their displaying. Curator Reem Fadda was quoted as saying,

> The mood now is that the artists don't need to explain themselves anymore. There is no need for anyone to explain or defend themselves. They are here to speak their minds, concerns, and anxieties that are universal. The artists have nothing to prove.
>
> (Proctor, 2022)

Again, the prominent positioning of women artists, including Saudis Shadia Alem and Dana Awartani and Emiratis Zeinab AlHashemi and Shaikha AlMazrou, sent a clear signal that the Kingdom provides an inclusive environment for women artists and creative professionals, at least in its most public-facing cultural arenas.

In December 2021, another contribution to the biennial calendar opened in Riyadh: *Feeling the Stones*, the first iteration of the Diriyah Contemporary Art Biennale. Curated by the director of Beijing's UCCA Contemporary Art Center, Philip Tinari,

> the biennial was established [in 2020] by the Saudi Ministry of Culture and is aimed at promoting the kingdom's cultural standing in the world, and at advancing Saudi Arabia as an 'open' society, as part of the government's Vision 2030 initiative.
>
> (Artforum, 2021)

As with Desert X AlUla, women are featured prominently in both curatorial roles and as exhibiting artists. Saudi researcher Wejdan Reda, who earned her MA in Curating Contemporary Art from the Royal College of Art in London served as one of the assistant curators for the biennial, providing an introduction for Tinari to local artists. According to Reda, one of the key benefits of the biennial is to "provide a platform for Saudi viewers and Saudi audiences to view works from around the world but in their home country", a tacit acknowledgment of the fact that while the Kingdom may be opening itself up to the outside, its citizens, particularly Saudi women, may not have the ability to travel to view contemporary art in international settings (Saleh, 2021). Saudi women artists featured in the Diriyah Biennale include some discussed previously in this volume, such as Manal Al-Dowayan, Zahrah Alghamdi, Maha Malluh, Lulwah Al-Homoud and Dana Awartani, as well as members of a younger generation such as Sarah Abu Abdallah and Ghada Al Hassan, whose monumental work *Horizontal Dimensions* (2021), an undulating canvas with abstract images in shades of yellow and gold, dominated its section of the galleries. Another emerging artist, Riyadh-based choreographer and dancer Sarah Brahim, presented a video work titled *Soft Machines/Far Away Engines* (2021), described by critic Stephanie Bailey (2022) as depicting "dancers enacting the morphology of breath, at times their interaction invoking queer intimacies through measured bodily entanglements." The phrase "queer intimacies" is not one that you would expect to encounter in a review of any public art exhibition held in Saudi Arabia; the presence of such a work may suggest that, as Melissa Gronlund (2021) notes, the hyperbole surrounding the Diriyah Biennale, with claims of its "game changing" status, may be "not far off. For the relatively isolated Saudi art scene, 2021/22 will be a moment of decisive shift."

UAE

The words and image of His Highness the late Sheikh Zayed bin Sultan al Nahyan, founder of the modern UAE and its first President, are seen everywhere in the Emirates. A prescient and thoughtful leader, Sheikh Zayed is often portrayed as ahead of his time on issues such as technological innovation, sustainability, climate and the role of women in society. The UAE has, particularly in the past 20 years or so, moved ahead of many of its Arab neighbors in affording paths to education and employment for its female citizens with the foundation of university programs and training schemes designed to attract and support Emirati women in establishing careers outside the home (Samier, 2015). While many women who choose to study and work after completing their higher education opt for careers in the government sectors, private and semi-government industries, including the arts and culture sector, are becoming more desirable destinations for young Emirati women professionals.

Zayed University

Zayed University, with campuses in both Dubai and Abu Dhabi, was founded in 1998 as one of the three government-sponsored higher education institutions in the country. As a federal university, Emirati students are provided their education at Zayed free of charge. It was the first institution in the UAE to offer a BFA degree (University of Sharjah began offering the BFA in 2020) and is the only federal institution to do so. Enrollment has grown substantially in recent years, with the degree programs in the College of Arts now enrolling over 800 students. The students in the BFA programs at Zayed University are all women, primarily Emirati, and thus are exactly the type of student the government rhetoric around supporting and encouraging the academic and professional growth of the country's women is aimed at. And, indeed, the university provides ample opportunities for such growth and development, through the classes and degree programs themselves, local and international field trip and exhibition opportunities, internship and mentorship programs and linkages with arts and cultural institutions throughout the UAE and the MENA region. And yet, while there are certainly success stories among Zayed University alumni, there are many recent graduates who report an inability to find meaningful employment or to pursue their artistic endeavors (Paschyn, 2013). Educators recognize that a crucial component of preparing students for success in their chosen field is providing them with

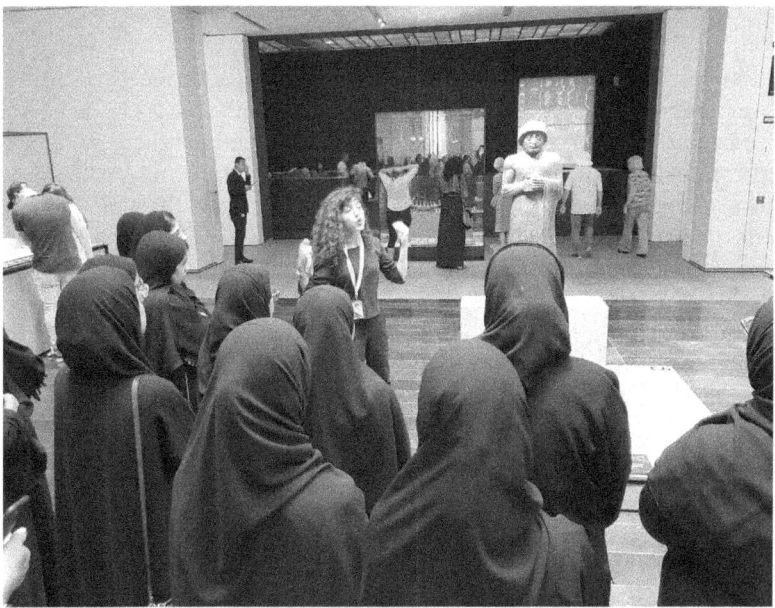

Figure 5.1 A group of Zayed University art and design students visiting the Louvre Abu Dhabi. Photograph by the author.

role models for that success. This is one of the reasons that institutions of higher education, particularly in the United States, have begun to push for more visibility of women and people of color in fields such as business and STEM: to encourage younger women with an interest and aptitude in those fields to, quite literally, see themselves in such professions. (Fisher et al., 2019) Young female students in the arts and design fields in the UAE have, at present, a much more limited landscape on which to model themselves and expatriate faculty who come to teach at universities such as Zayed frequently do not have the cultural knowledge and connections to immediately incorporate work by Arab, let alone Emirati, artists and designers (much less women) into their courses.

A 2019 Zayed University graduate, Aisha Al Ahmadi (n.d.), wrote of the disconnect felt by, at least some, students in the College:

> As a Middle Eastern woman, being aware of what art is and how essential it is and then to be conditioned with a Eurocentric view

of art history throughout my undergraduate education has been an unsettling experience to say the least.

In an environment where, as an expat, one is often concerned about overstepping cultural boundaries, even referencing works of Western women artists, particularly those with overtly feminist themes, can be uncomfortable. It takes time to learn the field, to build up the cultural familiarity that allows a teacher to introduce difficult themes and images in a way that interrogates tough issues while maintaining respect for cultural norms. In a transient environment such as the UAE, that time is not always available. Fortunately, this landscape seems to be changing. As more Emiratis, and other Gulf citizens, begin to attain advanced degrees and take up faculty positions in art, art history, architecture and design we might begin to see the regular incorporation of local role models for future art and design professionals.

Tashkeel

In 2007, Sheikha Lateefa bint Maktoum, a member of the ruling family of Dubai, graduated with a degree in fine arts from Latifa College, a self-contained fine arts facility managed by Zayed University, where Lateefa and ten other young women had been educated. The building, in the Nad Al Sheba neighborhood of Dubai, had been a supermarket, then a primary school, before its transformation into classrooms and studio spaces for painting, printmaking, photography and sculpture. When Lateefa and her cohort graduated, the original plan was to distribute the studio equipment among other entities and to repurpose the building yet again; however, Lateefa sought and obtained permission from the Ruler of Dubai, H.H. Sheikh Mohammed Bin Rashid Al Maktoum, to keep the art facilities in place and to transform the building into a hub for local artists, providing studio space, workshops, a library and exhibition space. The need for such a venue, which had no precedent in the UAE, was clear to Lateefa, a recently graduated artist:

> I didn't want the equipment to be dispersed across different entities because, at the time, I realized artists needed somewhere to create after graduating from university, besides working from home. Otherwise, they would simply stop working and take another career path because there was no public access to studios where they could continue their practice.

> (Tashkeel, 2018; p. 103)

Tashkeel opened in 2008 as a mixed-gender environment where any artist based in the UAE, Emirati or expatriate could apply for membership. The openness of the environment was radical for the time and place and critical to the success of Tashkeel over the years. Lateefa explains the significance of this mixed environment through the example of Tashkeel's annual open call exhibitions:

> Tashkeel, especially through its open calls, opens up the exploration of the current culture. As a result, you have different responses and a wider overview of the people living in the country. You get the expatriate's perspective, you get the local's perspective, you get the perspective of those who were born and raised here, which is completely different to those who have not grown up in Dubai. I like the fact that we do open calls for those living and working in Dubai – both Emiratis and expatriates. We receive surprising works including subject matter that we have never even thought about.
>
> (Tashkeel, 2018; p. 117)

Tashkeel also demonstrates its willingness to blur the boundaries between fine art and design through its support not only of individual graphic and product designers, many of whom have been members of Tashkeel since the early days, but also through programs such as Tanween, which each year takes a selected cohort of emerging UAE-based designers through a nine-month development program to take a product inspired by the surroundings of the UAE from concept to completion. In conjunction with the Critical Practice Programme, which provides mentorship to select UAE-based artists, the intent of Tanween, as described by Annabelle de Gersigny, an early employee of Tashkeel, is to "harness what is innate to the UAE; what comes naturally, what makes sense and what draws a place out of itself – breathing what is outside in, and releasing it back to the community" (Tashkeel, 2018; p. 165). Indeed, that description fits Tashkeel itself, as an organically developed, community-based arts institution that seeks to support the full breadth of the UAE's artists and designers in a way that foregrounds local knowledge and artistic production rooted in place, even if that place is as shifting and changeable as Dubai. This locally based institution offers a particularly important avenue for professional development for emerging women artists and designers, who are beginning to graduate in significant numbers from university programs but do not necessarily have access to international opportunities for further study, internships or employment.

SEAF

One of the challenges for contemporary artists in the UAE is the lack of post-graduate training programs in the fine arts within the country. While universities including Zayed University, American University of Sharjah, Sharjah University and, more recently, New York University Abu Dhabi, provide undergraduate training in the fine arts and design fields, only NYU Abu Dhabi offers a Master of Fine Art degree, which was inaugurated as recently as 2021. For local graduates, whether Emirati or expatriate, who wish to continue their education in the fine arts, studying for a master's degree abroad is the only option. However, for many Emirati women, studying abroad is not viable given family and cultural constraints. The Salama bint Hamdan Al Nahyan Emerging Artists Fellowship (SEAF), run by the Salama bint Hamdan Al Nahyan Foundation, in partnership with the Rhode Island School of Design (RISD), can provide an alternative for those artists.

Founded in 2013, the SEAF fellowship is a 10-month artistic education and development program that supports approximately 15 emerging UAE-based artists each year (like Tashkeel, this program is mixed-gender and includes both Emirati and long-term resident, expatriate, artists). Also like Tashkeel, SEAF was developed to meet the needs of emerging artists, to address "the specific challenges facing early career artists throughout the UAE, most notably a relatively undeveloped culture of constructive critique, access to artistic networks and the scarcity of affordable studio spaces" (BBC, n.d.). By partnering with RISD, the program affords access to a group of internationally connected faculty who mentor the participants through visits to Abu Dhabi, virtual consultations and, toward the end of the program, a two-week trip to the United States to visit the RISD campus as well as galleries and museums in New York. It is this back-and-forth engagement with US-based faculty that sets SEAF apart and provides fellows with the critical skills needed to, as RISD faculty member Anais Missakian explains, "analyze how their work has shifted since entering the SEAF program and instill in them new conceptual and formal goals for an investigative practice, whether or not they decide to pursue an MFA" (RISD, n.d.). For students who do wish to pursue an MFA degree, these are funded by the Foundation after completion of the SEAF program. The program can function as an intermediate step for students, perhaps easing family concerns about further education abroad, as well as an alternative to post-graduate education for those who are unable to travel outside of the UAE.

Warehouse 421

Two years after the establishment of SEAF, in 2015 the Salama bint Hamdan Al Nahyan Foundation established Warehouse 421 in Abu Dhabi, an exhibition and workshop space "committed to supporting emerging talent from the UAE, Middle East, and South Asia [and taking] a collaborative approach to hosting and curating exhibitions, presenting and contextualizing local and regional research, and examining cultural practices" (Warehouse 421, n.d.). Warehouse 421 serves as the location for the final critique and public exhibition of each SEAF cohort, as well as presenting a range of exhibitions, primarily showcasing work by UAE-based artists. In addition to its exhibition and public education programs, Warehouse 421 also sponsors a series of grants and professional development programs for artists from the MENASA region. These "capacity building" programs are designed to support the growth of the arts sector in Abu Dhabi and "continue to evolve from insights identified through focus groups and studying the response to Warehouse 421's general public programs" (Warehouse 421, n.d.).

One of these programs, the Curatorial Development Exhibition Programme, led to the 2021–2022 exhibition "As We Gaze Upon Her," curated by the Banat Collective, which presented a complex consideration of issues of gender and identity in Middle East society. Emiratis Sara bin Safwan and Sarah Alagroobi, who are the curatorial team behind the Banat Collective since 2016, created the group show as the culminating project of their work with the program. Their curatorial statement frames the exhibition as "expand[ing] the notion of 'woman', often constrained by social, cultural and existential insecurities and to investigate 'woman' as both an idea and a body" (Chaves, 2021). While this may not sound like a revolutionary brief, the exhibit marked the first of its kind in the UAE to present these themes as the main focus of the works displayed. Alagroobi explains, "We wanted to introduce concepts that had already been spoken about in the private sphere, but bring them out in public. The artworks showcase existing women's struggles today" (Hamdan, 2022). The support of Warehouse 421 and, by extension, the imprimatur of the Salama Bint Hamdan Al Nahyan Foundation are significant in the ongoing efforts by Emirati artists and curators to engage with the progressive and culturally sensitive themes of gender roles, heteronormativity and patriarchy addressed by the artists in this exhibition.

References

Al Ahmadi, A. (n.d.). 'Intellectual decolonization in Emirati art: A process of learning and unlearning'. [Online] Available at: https://101.art/blogs/research/intellectual-decolonization-in-emirati-art-a-process-of-learning-and-unlearning-by-aisha-al-ahmadi [Accessed February 21, 2022].

Al-Yahyai, F. (2012). 'The history of Omani women in the arts'. *The International Journal of Arts Theory and History*, 7(1), pp. 1–20. DOI: 10.18848/2326–9952/CGP/v07i01/36240

Art Kuwait. (2015). 'Opening of Abolish 153 at CAP'. [Online] Available at: http://artkuwait.org/2015/05/opening-of-abolish-153-at-cap.html [Accessed February 28, 2022].

Bailey, S. (2022). 'At Diriyah Biennale, Chinese history meets a Saudi future'. *Ocula*, January 12, 2022. [Online] Available at: https://ocula.com/magazine/features/diriyah-biennale/ [Accessed February 25, 2022].

BBC. (n.d.). 'Championing art at its grass roots'. [Online] Available at: https://www.bbc.com/storyworks/travel/abu-dhabi-unwrapped/championing-arts-at-its-grass-roots [Accessed February 24, 2022].

CAP. (2020). 'About'. [Online] Available at: https://www.capkuwait.com/about [Accessed February 28, 2022].

Chaves, A. (2021). 'Review: New Abu Dhabi art show aims to challenge how we define womanhood'. *The National*, October 20, 2021. [Online] Available at: https://www.thenationalnews.com/arts-culture/art/2021/10/20/review-new-abu-dhabi-art-show-aims-to-challenge-how-we-define-womanhood/ [Accessed February 24, 2022].

Edge of Arabia. (n.d.). 'Story'. [Online] Available at: http://edgeofarabia.com/about [Accessed February 25, 2022].

Edge of Arabia. (2008). 'Contemporary art from Saudi Arabia: Exhibition guide'. [Online] Available at: http://edgeofarabia.com/exhibitions/edge-of-arabia-london [Accessed February 25, 2022].

Fire Station. (n.d.). 'Artist in residence'. [Online] Available at: https://www.firestation.org.qa/en/artists-in-residence-programme [Accessed February 28, 2022].

Fisher, A. J. et al. (2019). 'Structure and belonging: Pathways to success for underrepresented minority and women PhD students in STEM fields'. *PLoS One*, 14(01), pp. 1–14. DOI: 10.1371/journal.pone.0209279

Gronlund, M. (2021). 'Saudi Arabia's cultural scene is in a moment of decisive shift'. *The Art Newspaper*, December 14, 2021. [Online] Available at: https://www.theartnewspaper.com/2021/12/14/escape-from-the-dark-ages-saudi-arabia-launches-its-first-biennial [Accessed February 25, 2022].

Hamdan, S. (2022). 'The Banat collective's latest exhibition is a bold depiction of womanhood'. *Arab News*, January 6, 2022. [Online] Available at: https://www.arabnews.com/node/1999186/lifestyle [Accessed February 24, 2022].

Kluijver, R. (2013). 'Contemporary art in the gulf: Context and perspectives'. [Online] Available at: https://issuu.com/robertk1/docs/contemporary_art_in_the_gulf_for_pr [Accessed February 16, 2022].

Mater, A. (n.d.). 'Development of the Saudi art scene from 1960'. [Online] Available at: https://www.ahmedmater.com/essays/development-of-the-saudi-art-scene-from-1960 [Accessed February 24, 2022].

Milliard, C. (2014). 'Is Qatar's $1 billion art spending not enough?'. *Artnet News*, June 3, 2014. [Online] Available at: https://news.artnet.com/art-world/is-qatars-1-billion-arts-spending-not-enough-32425 [Accessed February 28, 2022].

NYUAD. (2022). 'Khaleej Modern: Coming fall 2022'. [Online] Available at: https://www.nyuad-artgallery.org/en_US/our-exhibitions/main-gallery/khaleej-modern/ [Accessed February 16, 2022].

Paschyn, C. M. (2013). 'Women in the Gulf: Better educated but less employed'. *Al-Fanar Media*, October 16, 2013. [Online] Available at: https://www.al-fanarmedia.org/2013/10/women-in-the-gulf-better-educated-but-less-employed/ [Accessed February 24, 2022].

Proctor, R. A. (2022). 'In Saudi Arabia, a calm, meditative biennial defies the uproar as Desert X AlUla organizers say the "dust is settling" on the controversial show'. *Artnet News*, February 14, 2022. [Online] Available at: https://news.artnet.com/art-world/desert-x-alula-2022-2071844 [Accessed February 25, 2022].

RISD. (n.d.). 'Supporting cross cultural engagement'. [Online] Available at: https://www.risd.edu/news/stories/supporting-cross-cultural-engagement [Accessed February 24, 2022].

RUW. (n.d.). 'College of art and design'. [Online] Available at: https://www.ruw.edu.bh/?q=college-art-design-1 [Accessed February 24, 2022].

Saleh, H. (2021). 'Co-curator Wejdan Reda discusses goals of Saudi's first contemporary art biennale'. *Arab News*, November 22, 2021. [Online] Available at: https://www.arabnews.com/node/1972936/lifestyle [Accessed February 25, 2022].

Sultan Gallery. (n.d.). 'A brief history of the Sultan Gallery'. [Online] Available at: https://www.sultangallery.com/new-page [Accessed February 25, 2022].

Tashkeel. (2018). *Reference Point: A History of Tashkeel and UAE Art.* Dubai: Tashkeel.

Warehouse421. (n.d.). 'About'. [Online] Available at: https://www.warehouse421.ae/en/about/ [Accessed February 24, 2022].

Yee, V. (2020). 'Art rises in the Saudi desert, shadowed by politics'. *The New York Times*, February 11, 2020. [Online] Available at: https://www.nytimes.com/2020/02/11/arts/design/Desert-X-AlUla-saudi-arabia.html [Accessed February 25, 2022].

Index

For Product Safety Concerns and Information please contact our EU
representative GPSR@taylorandfrancis.com
Taylor & Francis Verlag GmbH, Kaufingerstraße 24, 80331 München, Germany

www.ingramcontent.com/pod-product-compliance
Lightning Source LLC
Chambersburg PA
CBHW070425180526
45158CB00017B/754